College Admissions Policies for the 1970s

Papers delivered at
the Colloquium on College Admissions Policies,
Interlochen, Michigan, June 18-23, 1967

College Entrance Examination Board, New York
1968

Copies of this book may be ordered from College Entrance Examination Board, Publications Order Office, Box 592, Princeton, New Jersey 08540. The price is $3 per copy.

Editorial inquiries regarding this book should be addressed to Editorial Office, College Entrance Examination Board, 475 Riverside Drive, New York, New York 10027.

Contents

Authors v

Clyde Vroman:
Introduction vii

Clyde Vroman:
Problems and Issues Confronting the Admissions Community 1

B. Alden Thresher:
Frozen Assumptions in Admissions 9

John F. Morse:
The Effect of Federal Programs on Admissions Policies 23

Charles W. Sanford:
State Plans for Higher Education and Their Influence on Admissions . 40

John D. Millett:
Clear Institutional Objectives Essential to Admissions Function . . 52

Edmund J. Gleazer Jr.:
Recognizing the Expanding Role of Junior Colleges in Higher
Education 66

Jack N. Arbolino:
Not the Traditional Student but Almost Everyone Else 84

Henry S. Dyer:
Recruiting the Disadvantaged: An Urgent Need 96

Albert G. Sims:
On the University, Admissions, and International Education 115

Theodore M. Newcomb:
Campus Environment as a Factor in Admissions 126

Dean K. Whitla:
Candidate Overlap Studies and Other Admissions Research 137

George H. Hanford:
A Look from the Twenty-first Century 166

Authors

Jack N. Arbolino
>   Executive Director, Council on College-Level Examinations
>   College Entrance Examination Board

Henry S. Dyer
>   Vice President, Educational Testing Service

Edmund J. Gleazer Jr.
>   Executive Secretary, American Association of Junior Colleges

George H. Hanford
>   Executive Vice President, College Entrance Examination Board

John D. Millett
>   Chancellor, Ohio Board of Regents

John F. Morse
>   Director, Commission on Federal Relations
>   American Council on Education

Theodore M. Newcomb
>   Professor of Sociology and Psychology, The University of Michigan

Charles W. Sanford
>   University Dean of Admissions and Records Emeritus
>   University of Illinois

Albert G. Sims
>   Vice President, College Entrance Examination Board

B. Alden Thresher
>   Director of Admissions Emeritus, Massachusetts Institute of Technology

Clyde Vroman
>   Director of Admissions, The University of Michigan

Dean K. Whitla
>   Director, The Office of Tests, Harvard University

Introduction

The growing importance, scope, and diversity of higher education in America, and indeed throughout the world, make it imperative and timely for colleges and universities in this country to give serious attention to the problems and issues inherent in their admissions policies, for these policies are the major factor in determining the ultimate size and makeup of their student bodies.

In 1957, the Fifth Annual Colloquium on College Admissions of the College Entrance Examination Board had as its topic, "Planning College Policy for the Critical Decade Ahead." In his Foreword to the published papers from the Colloquium, Hollace G. Roberts said:

" . . . these addresses make crystal clear the fact that there is no room for complacency in the admissions picture. And the implication arises again and again in the addresses that the prime responsibility for the establishment of a clearly stated, educationally and philosophically sound admissions policy, along with its interpretation and its practical and ethical application, rests squarely on the shoulder of the college admissions officer."[1]

The decade since 1957 has been memorable. That was the year of Sputnik I. The Advanced Placement Program was beginning to hit its expansive stride. Then in 1964 the first "tidal wave" of students reached the colleges, many of which were ill-prepared to meet their admissions problems. The past decade indeed has been a period of tremendous growth and evolutionary change in American education.

This invitational Colloquium on College Admissions Policies, co-sponsored by the College Board and The University of Michigan, brought together 80 professional admissions officers from all over the country in order to lay a foundation of ideas, information, and perspectives to be used in planning for the decade ahead. The *purposes* of the Colloquium were to help undergraduate admissions officers and administrators:

Understand the social, psychological, and educational significance of their responsibilities.

Understand the growing diversity and complexity of higher education at the campus, state, and national levels.

Assess and improve their admissions policies and practices.

---

1. *Planning College Policy for the Critical Decade Ahead.* New York: College Entrance Examination Board, 1958, p. vi.

Give leadership and assistance to their superiors—faculties, college officers, and governing boards—in the formulation and implementation of college admissions policies.

Build admissions policy structures that will be appropriate for the decade ahead.

The major *rationale* for the Colloquium was, first, the belief that the foundation of a successful college admissions program begins with the policies that govern its operation and, second, the belief that the admissions officer is primarily responsible for the creation of desirable and effective admissions policies for his institution.

The procedural method of the Colloquium revolved around prepared papers presented by nationally known authorities on topics of key importance to planning college admissions policies for the decade ahead. Those papers constitute the body of this publication. It is hoped that the reader will gain, as did the participants in the Colloquium at Interlochen, new insights into the evaluation and improvement of his or her institution's admissions policies and criteria for the decade ahead.

Members of the Colloquium Committee were Robert L. Jackson, director of admissions, Oberlin College; Hollace G. Roberts, director, Midwestern Regional Office of the College Board; Charles W. Sanford, dean of admissions and records, University of Illinois; Rixford K. Snyder, director of admissions and financial aids, Stanford University; and B. Alden Thresher, director of admissions emeritus, Massachusetts Institute of Technology.

Clyde Vroman

Chairman, Colloquium Committee
Director of Admissions, The University of Michigan

Problems and Issues Confronting the Admissions Community

Clyde Vroman

There are many complex and growing problems and issues in the planning of undergraduate admissions policies for this country's colleges and universities, be they public or private, large or small, old or new. Eleven major problem areas that have important implications for planning appropriate and effective college admissions policies for the decade ahead are presented below.

1. *College enrollments.* A recent report, *Projections of Educational Statistics to 1975-76*,[1] points out that, whereas by 1975-76 the overall school enrollment in the United States will increase by 12 percent, the projected jump in college enrollment is 49 percent. Colleges and universities are expected to enroll about nine million degree-seeking students in 1975-76, compared with 6.1 million enrolled in 1966-67. Figures 1 and 2, from that report, show graphically the predicted impact of population growth on American institutions of higher learning.

To some colleges and universities the deluge of students predicted particularly in Figure 2 implies enrollment indigestion as those institutions face the depressing problems of too many applicants. For other institutions, which have needed more applicants, it is a promised land overflowing with abundant numbers of potential students. To public institutions that attempt to serve first a particular group of students it brings a new set of problems in selectivity and admissions priorities. For private institutions, both large and small, it accents and stimulates old and new problems of roles, programs, and policies.

For some time private institutions have expressed alarm at the declining proportion of college students they enroll. And yet, by the U.S. Office of Education projections, the total opening fall degree-credit enrollment in private higher education will increase from the actual enrollment in 1965 of 1,901,883 to 2,680,000 in 1975. This is an increase of approximately 40 percent in 10 years. There are two major problems here. Does the private education sector want to expand this much? And, can private education find the funds to expand to this extent? The basic issue probably is what proportion of higher education

---

1. U.S. Office of Education (OE-10030-66). Washington: U.S. Government Printing Office, 1966, 113 pp.

1

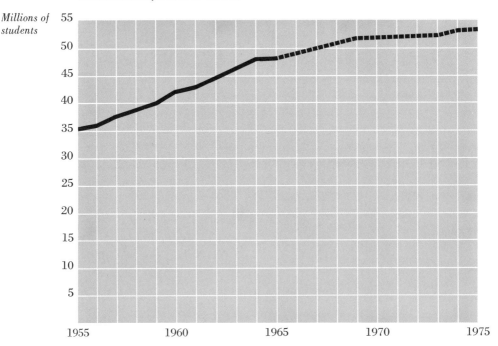

Figure 1. Fall Enrollment in Grades K-12 of Regular Day Schools: United States, 1955 to 1975.

should be served through private education in order that it may effectively make its unique contribution to education in this country.

Understanding national trends in population growth and college enrollment of course is only a first step in establishing a base of probable demand for enrollment in a particular college or university. It is much more important to identify the facts related to the segments of society from which the institution presently draws, and in the future may draw, its students. In any event, college enrollments will be affected significantly by the population trends, and these trends should be a primary factor in setting admissions policies in most colleges and universities.

2. *Improved secondary school education.* Secondary education has made dramatic improvements in the past two decades. In addition to recognizing the significant concept of individual differences in students, schools have added the functional approach of diversity of programs, depth of learning, and flexible rates of progress. The better secondary schools are achieving phenomenal results in preparing their stu-

2

Figure 2. Total Opening Fall Degree-credit Enrollment in
All Institutions of Higher Education: United States, 1955 to 1975.

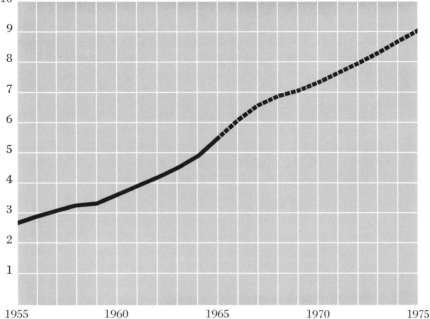

dents for college, even to the extent of offering considerable first-year
college work.

The problems and challenges emerging from this unusual development in education are substantial. How can admissions officers in their
respective colleges and universities understand and capitalize on these
changes in the high schools? How can they effectively assess the qualities and achievements of their applicants? How can they decide who is
qualified, or best qualified, for their institutions? How can they articu-
late their college offerings with the achievements of the secondary
schools? How can they best place and induct new students into college
instructional programs and into college methods of learning and teaching?

These and many similar problems and issues are fundamental in
planning college admissions policies. They lead to such concrete problems as academic course requirements for admission, the functions and
uses of standardized tests, the relevance of various admissions factors,

3

the quantity and quality control of student admissions, and the evaluation of the admissions policies and processes.

3. *The growth of junior colleges.* The fastest growing segment of education today is the two-year junior college. Not only are junior colleges expanding in numbers, they also are improving in quality and achievements. Through their national organization, the American Association of Junior Colleges, they are carrying out extensive and effective research and professional activities.

This relatively new development brings significant issues and problems to the senior colleges and universities. For example do the senior institutions have an obligation to serve the junior college graduates? Do they wish to render this service? If so, what policies, requirements, criteria, and processes will best undergird the selection and placement of these transfer students? What priorities in admissions should be given the junior college graduates who must transfer to continue their education? Most of the problems colleges encounter in admitting freshmen are also met in admitting transfer students. In addition, the problems of advanced credits, induction into curricular programs of study, and graduation on time call for astute and effective admissions policies and procedures in the senior colleges.

4. *Expansion of educational opportunities.* American higher education is rapidly changing its traditional character based on four years of undergraduate study leading to the baccalaureate degree and the completion of "education for life and livelihood." The country is witnessing a "takeoff" that is rapidly transforming many of the goals and programs of its colleges and universities. The institutions are looking for a greater diversity in the academic and personal characteristics of their new students; they are striving to find and serve minority groups who have been educationally and otherwise disadvantaged; they are attempting to meet the educational needs of adults who wish to return to formal studies; and they are extending their instructional services to people "where they are." Continuing education is rapidly becoming as important to the society and its citizens as the car is to the family. Already one fourth of all Americans are enrolled in formal educational programs, and the proportion of students will continue to grow in the years ahead.

Thus, while there will always be a fundamental place in higher education for the traditional undergraduate programs, their character is changing and will continue to change at an accelerated rate. Such changes bring a challenging new set of problems and issues in college

4

admissions policies. Failure to meet these needs will be a tragic dereliction in terms of human values and national security.

5. *Assessment of abilities and knowledge.* Functionally this assessment means the use of standardized tests in the counseling, selection, and placement of students in educational programs. Most admissions officers are accustomed to the traditional and routine functions and uses of existing tests. However, only a minority of admissions officers are at home in some of the newer areas of testing, as for example the new standardized tests that measure college-level achievement. And few if any can claim competency in the more esoteric areas of testing such as personality and motivation.

It seems clear that in the years ahead there will be more, not less, testing. As we admissions officers deal with increased ranges of individual differences, with divergent personal backgrounds, with the products of unconventional educational programs, and with new types of reasons and motivation for education, we must turn to new tools of measurement for the information we need. Otherwise, we will tend to fall back on the hard-core, structured system of years of education, credits, and grades. These are still important for students flowing normally through the educational system. But to use only these traditional devices on the atypical person would be unfortunate indeed. Probably no segment of college admissions policies contains more problems, issues, and opportunities for progress than does testing.

6. *Accreditation.* One of the most frequently misunderstood concepts in American education is "accreditation." This is a concept indigenous and unique to education in the United States. No other country in the world uses it as this one does to any extensive degree. First used in 1870 and developed rapidly around 1900, it became the main symbol of quality education and acceptability of preparation for college throughout most of the country. The six regional accrediting associations that serve the 50 states contain both secondary schools and colleges. Their original purposes had to do mainly with the articulation of schools and colleges, and this is still a basic objective.

In their early days the accrediting associations, like the preparatory schools, were concerned mainly with students going to college. With the advent of mass education in the 1930s, they assisted in the creation and development of the comprehensive high school, an institution for "all the children of all the people." The expansion of the American junior college to the mass-education level in the last decade is the college-level counterpart of the comprehensive secondary schools. This un-

5

precedented expansion of educational opportunities, unmatched in any other country of the world, was led and served substantially by the dedicated activities of the voluntary, regional accrediting associations.

Most people still assume that the primary function of these associations is to validate students' readiness for college. This has long since ceased to be the primary purpose of accreditation. The major purpose of accreditation now is to help establish and maintain high-quality schools and colleges that will do everything possible to develop and educate every one of their students. This does not mean that their products will be equal or even similar in ability and achievement; it means that it is hoped each student will have access to an educational environment and opportunity appropriate for him. To measure the differences in these products effectively colleges must utilize standardized testing.

What then is the role of accreditation in relation to college admissions policies? It is as an indication that a school or college is a reliable and reputable institution, not for profit, based on an acceptable educational philosophy and curriculum, and providing adequate opportunities for the educational development of the students it serves. When a student has had his secondary education in an unaccredited school, admissions officers have no validated evidence of ability and achievement except the results obtained by standardized testing. Unfortunately students from unaccredited colleges have been able to provide little reliable and interpretable evidence of educational achievement. The new College-Level Examination Program of the College Entrance Examination Board gives promise of providing a method of measuring these unknowns in ability and accomplishment.

One of the growing demands on the accrediting associations at the college level is to assist in the development of new colleges in this period of great expansion in higher education. The availability of federal funds for new facilities and programs for colleges and universities, provided they are accredited or approved by the regional accrediting association, has created a significant new role for these associations.

Clearly the area of accreditation contains a number of problems and issues basic to the refinement of admissions policies for every college or university.

7. *The expanding role of the federal government.* The federal government has become a major factor in American education and in most colleges and universities. Its main role so far has been to provide funds. But along with funds for scholarships and other financial aid, and for programs, facilities, and research, have come proscriptions, supervi-

6

sion, and the beginnings of external controls. This national movement is accelerating the extension of educational opportunities to diversified segments and age groups of the people. Inevitably these changes will call for revised and perhaps new admissions policies. Admissions officers need to know the current situation, the implications, and the probabilities for the future in this area. The problem is, "What admissions policies will be most appropriate to utilize constructively this new member of the American higher education family?"

8. *The growth of statewide systems of higher education.* A number of the states now have statewide systems of higher education, and several other states are about to launch similar reorganizations. This growing movement has significant implications for the admissions policies and practices of individual institutions. How can the institutions identify these new problems and devise their solutions in time to avoid most unfortunate results? What are some of the acceptable solutions to these problems?

9. *Foreign students.* Students from foreign lands have become a significant factor in the student bodies of the majority of American colleges and universities. Over 80,000 of them are in the country now, and this number will increase. Each institution of higher education should decide the role it wants to play in educating foreign students and what admissions policies will best carry out this role.

10. *Admissions research.* Both basic and evaluative research are essential for the formulation and administration of college admissions policies, and admissions officers must accept this responsibility to an increasing degree. They need first to know what kinds and amounts of research are necessary and desirable to undergird and assess their institution's admissions policies. What should be the nature and scope of such research? The 1967 College Board publication, *Research Guidelines for High School Counselors,*[2] prepared by the Experimental Designs Committee of the Association for Counselor Education and Supervision, seems to call for a similar publication for college admissions officers.

11. *Student characteristics and campus environments.* For many years psychologists have studied the problems of identifying student characteristics and relating these factors to the educational and social context of the campuses. Admissions officers seriously seek help in this area. Is it possible to select students in such a way as to improve their

---

2. New York, 114 pp.

adjustment to campus environments? Is there a positive relationship between student characteristics and campus environment? If so, how can admissions policies accomplish this end?

The 11 problems and issues listed above are only a sampling of the challenges to be faced in planning desirable and effective college admissions policies. The college admissions officer, if he truly fulfills his professional roles and functions, can and should play a major part in the formulation of college admissions policies. It is the role of the governing board and the faculty to decide what the educational aims and programs of the college or university will be, and it is their function to authorize the admissions policies that are designed to carry out the institution's mission. But the job of formulating and recommending desirable admissions policies should be carried out professionally by the admissions officer. What he does about these problems will have significant influence on the quality and achievements of his college or university.

8

Frozen Assumptions in Admissions

B. Alden Thresher

My purpose, as one no longer in the active admissions field, is not to give admissions people practical pointers, but rather to ask questions to which none of us fully knows the answers. I want to disturb and disquiet these people as I find myself disturbed and disquieted looking back on many of the practices I so confidently carried on during 25 years of selective admissions. So these remarks are really "The Confessions of a Reformed Admissions Officer."

The world of higher education is an intensely competitive one—competitive very often with respect to the wrong things, and often to the detriment of the student and of the public welfare. The College Entrance Examination Board, cosponsor of this conference, has as its province a group of limited areas in which the interests of competing institutions, by some happy chance, run parallel, so that joint action is possible and mutually sought after, and competition if not absent is at least muted. In the African big game country, in time of drought, there is said to be a kind of truce among the animals by which all come to the water hole, lions and antelopes alike, made peaceable by their mutual need for water. So the College Board has found a useful niche by doing jobs in which the otherwise competitive interests of colleges and universities run parallel through a common need to get certain things done. The Board, like the United Nations, has no coercive powers, but serves as a forum, and as an agency to conduct programs that all the members agree are needed. But the Board can do little to mitigate the competitive forces in areas where these interests conflict.

I have found it useful to look at the problem of college admissions on three levels of analysis.[1] Level One represents the interest of the individual student in finding a college that suits his needs, and in getting into it. This he does with a sharp eye to his own future. Level Two represents the problem of the individual college in attracting and selecting students. The college has an even sharper eye, however, in furthering what it conceives (sometimes mistakenly) to be its own interests, and these may conflict with the ultimate needs and welfare of the student and of the public. Level Three, the one that I wish to emphasize today,

---

1. See B. Alden Thresher, *College Admissions and the Public Interest.* New York: College Entrance Examination Board, 1966, 93 pp.

9

deals broadly with admissions in the light of the public interest. In this context, to paraphrase the words of a late, distinguished son of Michigan, it does not necessarily follow that what is good for College X is good for the United States.

I ask admissions officers to look with me, *philosophically*, at some of the broad problems of education that impinge upon admissions. To look at a subject philosophically means, in the words of William James, "the habit of always seeing an alternative, of not taking the usual for granted, of making conventionalities fluid again, of imagining foreign states of mind." The human race has always had a remarkable capacity for taking for granted whatever it has got used to. We tend to regard the familiar as being *ipso facto* reasonable. And we are in a constant state of believing that we have arrived—that we have reached a state of enlightenment, that the ignorance of former ages has now been dispelled. We fail (in the words of Paul Tillich) "to approach knowledge with that astonishment which is the source of all knowledge."

I can illustrate this tendency by a sentence from Dr. John Hill, an eminent astronomer in eighteenth century London. In 1754 he wrote: "Astronomy is the science which teaches a knowledge of the stars and, in general, of all the heavenly bodies, their form, structure, appearances and motions; their place or situation in the heavens; their magnitude and their distance; a large and extensive field, but at this time greatly cultivated, so much, indeed, that very few improvements can be expected to be hereafter made in it, very little being unknown that it proposes to teach."[2]

This reminds me of the little boy in A. A. Milne's verse:
"Now I am six, I am clever as clever
So I think I'll be six for ever and ever."

What I am trying to convey is that the field of education, so far from being understood, is still in a primitive stage, but that we may well be on the verge of immense changes, which will explosively disarrange our easy and somnolent preconceptions. We cannot afford to assume that what we cannot explain does not exist, nor that the protean potentialities of the human mind will long rest satisfied with what now passes for education. It would be rash to predict or prophecy, but I want to transmit, if I can, my own sense of vast, impending change. Nobody can keep fully abreast of all current developments, but the effort to do so

2. Quoted in "Thomas Wright's Astronomical Heritage," in *The Scientific Adventure*, by Herbert Dingle. London: Pitman, 1952, p. 119.

10

sharpens our sensibilities and our intuition. A friend once asked Alfred de Musset if he was working on a new novel. De Musset replied, "One doesn't work, one listens." So some part of our time may well be used to listen—to listen with the third ear, if one wishes, to some of the signs of the times.

If we look broadly at education, even in modern times (say the last 300 years) we find it has been formal, ceremonial, pedantic, tradition-bound, often to the point of being truly fossilized in an almost literal sense; it has stressed rote learning; it has been hedged by barriers of social class and ascribed status; it has been the perennial vehicle of snobbery (along with dress, occupation, residence, accent, and much else); it has been more often than not irrelevant to the student's needs (it was Dorothy Parker who said: "The only thing I learned in school that helped me in later life was that if you spit on a pencil eraser it will erase ink"); it has usually been confused with indoctrination and inter-mixed with it; it has usually been authoritarian, and it has often been brutal.[3] As a recent addition to this list of horrors, we might add a strong tendency to chronological rigidity—the idea that all students should follow a uniform lockstep through school and college.

I think we are now coming into an era of change and innovation. The ice is breaking up in the river (or just beginning to break up), and fresh ideas are beginning at least to get a hearing and a trial. In particular four major trends seem to me significant.

1. We have grasped the idea that talent, to a much greater degree than anyone realized, is not something stumbled upon and found, here and there; it is an artifact, something that can be produced. This is a completely revolutionary idea, which reverses all the thinking that had guided the European and British universities from their inception. It is remarkable that the 1963 "Robbins Report" in Britain[4] specifically disclaims the "pool of ability" theory—the idea that only a small fraction of the population is capable, under any circumstances, of coping with higher education. This elitist view led to the conclusion that "more means worse."

2. We are beginning to see education as a continuum of life-long

---

3. Nineteenth century biography is replete with horrible examples. One of the most striking, Sir Oliver Lodge's *Past Years, An Autobiography* (London: Hodder & Stoughton, Ltd., 1931), is worth reading, if only to gain the impression that education does move ahead.
4. *Higher Education*, Report of the Committee appointed by the Prime Minister under the Chairmanship of Lord Robbins. London: H. M. Stationery Office, 1963, 335 pp.

duration, a notion that tends to soften and dissolve much conventional thinking. It means that at one extreme the key importance of infancy and preschooling is at last getting to be recognized, and at the other extreme, life-long, adult education is on the way to becoming a norm rather than an exception. So we see that the present breaking points between educational stages are essentially arbitrary, resulting from a mixture of historical accidents and administrative convenience. Just as some California towns rest uneasily upon the San Andreas Fault, so the admissions business rests, no less uneasily, upon the tradition of a break, a redistribution and switching point, or, if one prefers, a major traffic interchange between the twelfth and thirteenth grades. It seems a healthy tendency that this sharp boundary is beginning to be eroded from both sides. The idea of education as a continuum reinforces the idea that tests are increasingly seen as diagnostic guidance devices, the main purpose of which is to help the student, to speed him on his way, or at the very least to bring him up to par. All education, in one sense, is remedial education. Low marks or low test scores, seen in this light, are passports to more (and better) learning, not instruments of exclusion from opportunity to learn.

3. We have made at least a start in some radical new curriculums, but it would be a mistake to think it will stop there. New approaches to the learning process, more fundamental than rearrangements of subject matter, are in the making. The forces of innovation have been more active below the college level than at the college level. This, by itself, portends explosive changes in higher education in general, and in admissions in particular.

4. Educators are perhaps beginning to look more broadly at the spirit of the times and less narrowly at what they have thought of as their little realm of formal instruction. One sign of this is the powerful educational effect of mass media. More broadly, there is a parallel between recent innovations in education and the newer tendencies in the art of management; I mean management in the broadest meaning of the word, whether it is business management, government administration, or the conduct of a military or a religious organization.

The classic model for all these administrative tasks has been bureaucracy in the technical sense. This is a pyramidal structure, with sharply defined limits of responsibility and authority. In it, authority flows downward from the top. Information may flow upward from the bottom, but never policy, initiative, or wisdom. This model is not to be underestimated, for it has held human affairs together for centuries. At

12

its best, say in the civil service of the eighteenth century German states or nineteenth century Britain, it has worked well.

Contemporary thinking, represented, for example, by the late Douglas McGregor[5] and by Warren Bennis, and by much of the newer management training, sees this model as far too rigid and limited. It is uneconomical because it enlists only a small fraction of the energy, good will, ingenuity, and cooperativeness inherent in most people; in fact it actively frustrates these impulses. The old model assumed that all workers were ignorant, and therefore in need of detailed instruction; lazy, and therefore in need of pushing; disorganized, and therefore in need of regimentation. It is now becoming apparent to enlightened managers that there is an immense reservoir of capability in most workers in any field that has been repressed, and converted into rebelliousness, by the bureaucratic management model.

It is not merely a coincidence that, as thinking changes in the management field, it is changing also in education. The conventional notion that students (of any age) are ignorant, and so need instruction; rebellious, and so need curbing; lazy, and so need the threat of failure, has begun to give way. Today's student unrest is in reality only a surface symptom of the powerful forces now stirring in the direction of a more enlightened view of education and of the learning process.

In the questions we ask, there lie embedded our presuppositions and our principles. It will be remembered that whenever Thorstein Veblen mentioned anyone's "principles" he always added, in parentheses, "habits of thought." Every epoch is characterized by the kind of questions it instinctively asks. Among all the variant views and systems that characterize our time, we need to look for the fundamental assumptions that all of these unconsciously presuppose. We search these to discover our real "habits of thought." These will be the assumptions so obvious that people do not know that they are assuming them, because no other way of putting the matter has ever occurred to them. So the last thing a fish would ever discover is the existence of water. Now, what are some of these presuppositions, these inarticulate major premises in college admissions? I would like to list a few; and I think it will be seen how they contrast with the broad trends sketched above.

1. The first inarticulate major premise is that the way the learning process is now organized is a valid, defensible norm. If a student does

5. Douglas M. McGregor, *The Human Side of Enterprise*. New York: McGraw-Hill Book Company, 1960, 246 pp.

not adjust to it, he is a failure. Education is defined as what the faculty has long been doing. Those who do not respond are, by definition, uneducable.

A corollary to this is the notion that there is some "one best way" to carry on instruction; find this one best way, and impose it on all. Emil Duclaux said: "Nature loves diversity; education aims at repressing it." Perhaps the saving feature of our higher education in this country is that it is so chaotic. Despite these tendencies to uniformity, some diversity creeps in, and a certain large diversity is enforced by the multiplicity of auspices under which our education is conducted. Somebody, somewhere, may occasionally do something right, if only inadvertently. Diversity is the mainspring of human progress, and our country is large enough and varied enough partly to counteract the powerful forces of uniformity.

2. There is the assumption that selection of students is of key importance, and that if some selection is good, more is better. The ambience in much of the admissions process is an atmosphere of grudgingly extending a valuable privilege to a small selected few. This has grown up partly through the assumptions of the "pool of ability" theory, partly because of the financial and physical impossibility of keeping up with the demand for education by providing more and bigger colleges and universities, and partly through the magic of "brand names" in higher education. The lag leaves us in a condition of scarcity, which looks chronic, if not indeed permanent.

A few advanced countries—New Zealand, the United States, perhaps Japan—may be able to get ahead within a generation to the point of making available higher education of appropriate kinds to all who want or need it. But for most of the world the shortage will be prolonged and tragic. Prolonged because neither staff nor equipment can catch up with the demand; tragic because education is a chief instrument of development, and without it poverty and inertia must continue to be the rule in the underdeveloped countries.

Even the so-called advanced countries of Europe are far behind in higher education. You are familiar, I am sure, with these statistics, but John Fischer sums them up in a nutshell. "The six Common Market countries, with a combined population about the same as that of the United States, are turning out only one-fifth as many college graduates. To put it another way, in America roughly one person out of every three in the college age-group actually is attending some institution of higher learning; while in England, for instance, the ratio is one in sev-

14

enteen and in Italy one in thirty."[6] The Dennison Report[7] demonstrated that the return on investment in education is at least as high as on other forms of investment, so that educational expenditures are in fact true, productive investments, not extravagance.

This lag in meeting the demand for education has a peculiarly stultifying effect on education in the more selective institutions. College faculties reason thus: if we are in such great demand, we must be pretty good. They are confirmed in the innate conservatism that has always been the bane of education.

3. There is an assumption that dropouts are a bad thing. The "collegiocentric" view, which regards the existing pattern as a proper norm, must view any departure from the conventional four-year pattern as a regrettable lapse; it is given an aura of failure. But there are colleges, to drop out of which is a sign of energy and determination. Such students are "climbouts," and deserve admiration, not censure. An adequate system of higher education would be organized to offer appealing versions of educational experience to the action-oriented student, who so often provides in later life the driving force of leadership in practical affairs, but who reacts adversely to passive study, or to learning for its own sake. We need, too, a much freer movement among colleges and universities, something like that which throughout the nineteenth century exerted a civilizing effect on generations of European students.

4. We assume that *prediction* is of first importance, because of our assumption that our own educational processes are an ideal norm. So we get a tight, closed circle of prediction (using school marks or tests or both) followed by selection, based on the prediction, followed by validation against grade-point averages, from which new prediction equations are generated, and the closed circle continues. We forget that the whole evaluation is based on a unidimensional scale of marks and test scores, which ignores the rich variety of human talent. The people who turn out 20 or 30 years later to have really left their mark on the life of their times will turn out to include a high proportion of individuals not identified by these predictive, selective processes. Among them will be many dropouts—but we never seem to learn. Dropouts have been a leading source of achievers for centuries, from Emily Dickinson to

6. "The Editor's Easy Chair," *Harper's*, May 1967, pp. 18, 21.
7. Edward F. Dennison, *The Sources of Economic Growth in the United States and the Alternatives Before Us* (Supplementary Paper). New York: Committee for Economic Development, 1962.

Robert Frost; from Michael Faraday and Charles Darwin to Winston Churchill. It is a long and illustrious list; its names are among the glories of art, literature, science, and commerce, but somehow we never look at it when we start operating our little college-centered prediction systems.

A number of colleges, sensing all this, have tried to go behind the conventional cycle of tests and marks. They have accepted a limited freshman delegation low on these formal indicia, but who show evidence of being "doers" or "achievers" or who are "interesting," "original," or "creative." All this is probably a step in the right direction. But it is not enough. Any judgment, whether by a faculty committee, an admissions officer, or anyone else, is bound to reflect the current, accepted scheme of values of the society. We all are optimistic enough to think we know a promising candidate when we see one. This assumption I seriously question. Some of the people we most need are the ones we would eliminate first, and automatically. As A. N. Whitehead put it, "Only certain kinds of excellence are possible in particular historical epochs." We don't even know what the full range of excellence might be, if our (necessarily) restricted notions are measured against the quite unfathomed possibilities of human talent.

The human race has a genius for overlooking clues that are right under its nose. For example the lodestone, or natural magnet, had been known for centuries before Faraday, as had some of the phenomena of static electricity. Here was the key to electromagnetic theory, which has completely revolutionized our views of the nature of matter and energy and of how the universe is put together, as well as revolutionizing our technology. Yet man persistently ignored these clues, because they seemed odd and exceptional in the then ruling concept of how the world was constituted. They did not fit our preconceived notions.

I have no doubt whatever that even more revolutionary knowledge will come to light about human talent and potentialities, and that what college admissions people are currently doing will look extremely silly, in the light of this later and fuller knowledge.

5. There is the assumption that one should assemble as many "good" students as possible in a given college. This presumably will result in more alumni achievement, and redound to the credit of all concerned. The difficulty with this principle, which has been widely followed, is twofold. First, it permits selection to take the place of educational reform. If one assembles a strong enough group of students, nothing the faculty does can hold them back much, and the faculty can take credit

16

for their achievements. This relieves the faculty of responsibility for improving the teaching process. Second, it has never been demonstrated that it is in the public interest to assemble all the high-powered students in a few selected colleges. For all we know, they might be more effectively utilized as radiant centers of stimulation and influence if scattered among other institutions, less prestigious and less overapplied to. The situation can be summarized by saying that we don't always know a promising student when we see one, and if we did, we might sometimes do better in the sight of God and in the light of public welfare to encourage him to go elsewhere.

6. The assumption is that the student who shines most brightly in high school, or on tests, or on some combination of the two, is the one to go far. The most searching critique of this assumption that I have seen has been made by the biologist, John T. Bonner.[8] His main point is this: the human animal at birth is the most helpless of any mammal, and has the longest dependent infancy. But this means a longer period of plasticity, learning, and mental growth. A young chimpanzee outdistances a human infant in rate of development for a year or two, but then stops, at a low ceiling, while the human infant retains the potentiality of growth for many years.

Now what we need most of all under modern conditions of rapid change are the kinds of people who can keep on growing for many years, and remain plastic in ability to learn and adapt. "Would not the ideal person," Bonner asks, "be one whose mind, no matter how laboriously in the beginning, never stops learning, never closes, never atrophies?" It is true that exceptional precocity may presage great genius, particularly in music, mathematics, and the physical sciences. It is also true that we do not at present know how to identify those who will retain longest the capacity for growth and plasticity. But Bonner's central point is that the kind of selection practiced by the selective colleges may actually be counterproductive. "It is hard to predict," he says, "what effect college life will have on any one person. For some, certainly, it is a place where they learn to glow, but now we are asking them to glow first." It would be ironic if those who don't "glow first" and who find their way into relatively "open door" colleges, should turn out, 30 years later, to be the real winners. Perhaps the selective colleges, by ignorant selection, are weakening themselves in relative terms, compared with

8. "A Biologist Looks at Unnatural Selection," *Princeton Alumni Weekly*, November 23, 1962, pp. 6-16.

17

those who come nearer to welcoming all comers. Bonner sees this at least as a real possibility.

It is perfectly clear that for the time being, the practical world being what it is, some selectivity has to be exercised at admission. The error seems to lie in thinking that if some selectivity is good, more selectivity is better, and that, by honing and sharpening our present quite imperfect selective measures, we can assemble classes that will grow continuously and indefinitely better.

7. There is an assumption that the achievements of alumni reflect credit on a college. Perhaps sometimes, and within limits, they do. But this effect is generally much overstated. What we need is a concept akin to that of the U.S. census of manufactures in estimating the "value added by manufacture." I hesitate to use an industrial analogy, because industrial processes are not, in general, appropriate analogues for the nurtural influences and organismic processes that are the essence of education. But it is nevertheless true that the forces of preselection and the image of particular colleges, sometimes reinforced by the college's own selective processes, may bring in a concentration of able students— so able that nothing the faculty does to them can slow them down appreciably. In such situations the college serves more as a marshaling yard for talent than as a generator of it. A. W. Astin's studies,[9] looking at large statistical samples of students that cut across the boundaries of particular institutions, have shown that these situations occur.

I have listed seven presuppositions that I believe underlie much of the conventional wisdom about college admissions. But if, following William James' thought, we look at the subject philosophically, these appear, not as immutable laws of nature, but as conventions that, though frozen, may yet be made fluid again—we look for alternatives where we had assumed there were none, we prepare ourselves to entertain hospitably states of mind that have been quite foreign to our habits of thought.

Instead of assuming that the "college-going" pattern we now know is fixed and final, we can conceive of a much wider range of educational patterns such as will stimulate a wider variety of temperaments. There will have to be many alternatives available, and multiple combinations of jobs and study. The "natural student" will get on with little help, but

---

9. See "Productivity of Undergraduate Institutions," *Science*, April 13, 1962, pp. 129-135. See also "Undergraduate Institutions and the Production of Scientists," *Science*, July 26, 1963, pp. 334-338.

the student who needs to see a coupling between knowledge and action will need different treatment. We shall see libraries of filmed and taped lectures and demonstrations instantly on tap, so that the faculty, relieved of much routine exposition, can spend more time on its real job of interacting with students—stimulating, encouraging, criticizing, needling, or brow-beating as the occasion demands.

Perhaps the art of college guidance may eventually be refined to the point where the student thinks, not of finding a college where something favorable will be done to him, or for him, or on his behalf—essentially a passive concept. His habit of mind will be centered on the *learning* process: how does one go about learning, using whatever tools come to hand. A student imbued with this viewpoint will not worry about "the college of his choice." He will pick up whatever aids to learning are available in whatever environment he finds himself, and go on from there. Our present educational vocabulary is full of passivity: one *takes* a course, one is *"given"* a good education. We can hope that in future students ready for higher education will think more in terms of tackling a subject, of exploring a field of study, of getting the answers to questions that they themselves ask. Good teaching and good guidance can generate these attitudes.

So the presupposition about selection may also change. Some qualifications must be insisted on, but it does not follow that super-selection will set us ahead. The processes of organic evolution rely heavily on chance and random effects. If, above some reasonable minimum of qualification, we were to draw the names of applicants out of a hat, we might stand a better chance of getting a well-assorted class than by our present ignorant and clumsy selection methods. The late Irwin Lorge made the perceptive remark that the only thing that makes the admissions process bearable is its large percentage of error. This is just another way of saying that a healthy degree of randomization has sneaked in by the back door. One day, perhaps, we shall learn to judge colleges by what they can do with a fairly average bright group of students, instead of judging them by what they can do if they are given all the breaks ahead of time.

Again, perhaps we shall learn to encourage some dropouts, climbouts, or floatouts. Here is an area in which colleges are invincibly self-centered. A student who needs a change of venue is likely to find himself tagged with an aura of failure, and to find the greatest difficulty getting into a college better suited to him. I look for an enlightened era in which part of a college's normal job will be to take at least some

19

transfers who have not responded well to their initial environment, and try on them a different set of stimuli. Success in this sort of experiment would entitle a college quite honestly to boast of the efficacy of its educational processes. Before that happy day comes, much effort will be needed to get our thinking into a broader frame than local and quite parochial loyalties and rivalries.

Perhaps, again, we may see less stress on the closed circle of prediction, selection, and validation that tends to confirm and intensify whatever scheme of education has taken hold. I commend to admissions officers Joshua Fishman's[10] thoughtful articles on criteria of success in education. I might go further and seriously question whether it is feasible to set up such criteria, or whether it is meaningful to talk at all about "success" in higher education. Exercises in defining the objectives and purposes of education are likely to turn into what Henry Dyer calls "word-magic," because education is essentially an open-ended operation whose final result, like that of research, cannot be foretold. Fortunately many things happen to students in college that no one, including those who may have tried to define the college's objectives, could have foreseen. A single year spent in college by a dropout can have incalculable influence on him. Are we to say that this is not a part of the college's job, or that it does not contribute to "success"? The word "success" may have a definable meaning in the restricted context of elementary education, or even in some definable aspects of vocational or professional education. But in the context of lifelong influence on the student, or on his ultimate significance to society, the meaning evaporates, or diffuses over the whole of society. Education, in its best sense, like research in its truest sense, is an exploration. If we talk about "success," we have to ask, "Compared with what?"

I need not belabor in detail all the assumptions that freeze our thinking. I have said enough to convey the main idea. We need, I think, a more sociological view of the admissions process. As we come into an era in which the majority of high school graduates will be continuing in some kind of further education, some of them for extended periods, we need to see admissions, not as a series of administrative devices, but as a social process by which the society moves a large segment of its youth into a wide range of educational experience. This ought to in-

---

10. See especially Joshua A. Fishman and Ann K. Pasanella, "College Admission–Selection Studies," *Review of Educational Research*, Vol. XXX, No. 4, October 1960, pp. 298-310. With bibliography.

clude its most energetic and promising segment. They will be self-identified in the fullness of time, but we delude ourselves if we think we can identify them all in advance.

In the past, whole populations have been far too patient with the scholarly arrogance of universities, partly because most young people had no wish to enter the kind of scholarly life that attracted only a tiny minority, and partly because an illiterate populace regarded universities with an awe and veneration born of ignorance. The university ethos was set first by the church in the tradition of monkish learning, then by the ruling groups in society. The United States was the first to breach this cultural barrier with a broadly based university system. The innocent pedantries of the faculty can still get in the way of education, but we have advanced beyond the European models that still match medieval regalia with medieval social attitudes.

But for all this, we have not yet learned how best to classify and group students for diagnosis and guidance in ways that bring diversity and stimulation. The rigid "college-going" stereotype has taken a deep hold on our folkways, and we have a hard time disentangling genuine educational values from meretricious consideration of "prestige."

We still think of tests primarily as hurdles, barriers, means of exclusion. It still requires an act of the imagination to look ahead to a time when it may no longer be necessary to separate the process of learning and the process of testing—the two may tend to coalesce into one integrated process as the possibilities of computer-assisted learning unfold. We must be willing to entertain the possibility that the pencil-and-paper test as we now know it may turn out to be merely an interim, empirical device that served a useful purpose in a period of transition. It is not at all inconceivable that learning and testing may become integrated into a single process.

The contemporary use of computers in education for such functions as scheduling and registration runs quite parallel to their use in banks, department stores, and the like. All these uses are legitimate and desirable as far as they go, but we must realize that they represent an extremely primitive, mechanical way of utilizing a device whose flexibility and ultimate potential far transcend anything we can now imagine. The possibilities of using electronic means of association, logic, and combinations of ideas go far beyond what we now think of as machines. The stereotype of the machine as a clanking, inhuman monster is wholly inappropriate to the subtle and powerful extensions of the mind that we may confidently expect in the years ahead through utilizing the pos-

21

sibilities of solid state physics and electronics. Insofar as tests now play a part in the admissions process, we may therefore expect to see startling changes, also, in the habits of thought that we bring to bear on admissions processes.

I believe that the future is full of hope, if we do not allow ourselves to become bogged down in the mass of day-to-day practical detail. There is a strong element of necessary logistics in admissions, which tends to load us with such details. We have made great progress in this country in spreading a wide net to catch talent, and have begun to grasp the fact that talent is in large measure something not that we just hunt for but that we can produce. We worry about articulation—fitting education at successive stages together so that the student does not on the one hand suffer from gaps in his knowledge or, on the other, find himself needlessly repeating something he has already mastered. We shall have to organize in a more flexible manner for this. It is peculiarly important in the areas of accumulative knowledge in which prerequisites and the sequential order of subject-matter treatment are important. Mathematics and science are typical of this area.

But it is interesting to observe that the educational systems that show the most perfect articulation between secondary school and university are usually the very ones that restrict higher education to a small fraction of the age group. In countries where this occurs, the secondary school becomes a tame appendage of the university system with the same limitation of numbers. There is no articulation problem, because the two are so closely linked. I believe that our much more broadly based even if more chaotic educational system holds far more hope for the future if we can bring into it some elements of order without subjecting it to the restrictions of an academic tradition more appropriate to an earlier time.

22

The Effect of Federal Programs on Admissions Policies

John F. Morse

In a way this colloquium is a reunion for me, and I undertake my assignment with a sense of nostalgia. Just 11 years ago I presented a paper at the College Board's first admissions colloquium at Arden House. And in preparing my present paper, I had occasion to look over that moldy manuscript to see what had happened to me, and to the world of higher education, in the intervening years.

On a clear day, from Arden House, one should have been able to see forever. What struck me on rereading my 1956 paper was the shortness, the myopia of my vision. During the entire course of the hour required to deliver it and the discussion that followed, there was not, with the exception of the 52-college NROTC officer-recruiting program, one mention of federal interest, federal activity, or federal funds. At that time, as far as education was concerned, they did not exist. Yet today, 11 years later, I doubt whether any institution represented at this colloquium can plan intelligently, determine its role, or, indeed, even have a role unless it considers carefully its relationship to the federal interest in higher education.

Before speculating on the shape of things to come, I should like to examine briefly some of the existing federal programs that may well influence college admissions policies more in the future than they have in the past. It is quite possible that all institutions and particularly private institutions must redesign those policies. The massive nature of federal programs is likely to make impossible a continued laissez-faire attitude or a policy of having no policy.

In retrospect I found myself wondering why in 1956 I made no mention of the GI Bill, for it was then an important factor in college admissions. The probable answer is that it had very little meaning for the reasonably selective, underendowed private institution. The World War II GI Bill had proved a boon to this very kind of institution, since it provided for the payment of tuition—whatever the fee might be—with an added payment to the student for subsistence. Sleepy, undernourished colleges that had previously led a hand-to-mouth existence found it possible to raise their charges markedly, upgrade faculty salaries and therefore presumably faculty quality, and often build buildings with their surplus income.

23

All of this, of course, was changed under the Korean War GI Bill, when a veteran received a flat payment out of which he had to pay both his fees and subsistence. For obvious reasons this change alone channeled most of the veterans into public institutions. It did not matter much then, for the numbers involved were small compared to the numbers demobilized after World War II, and in general the academic ability of the Korean War veteran was considerably lower than that of his predecessor, and he was, therefore, "less attractive." Those servicemen with high ability and strong motivation had, through student deferments, already completed their college education before they entered the service.

Now and for the future, however, this situation may well change. I would not try to predict what the changes will be, but I am certain that all admissions officers must pay more attention in the future than they have in the past to Selective Service patterns and to the nature of the flow of men into and out of the military. The GI Bill seems certain to be a permanent piece of legislation, and its benefits are likely to be increased as the years go on, if only to create an inducement to voluntary enlistment. We are not likely ever again to provide a separate provision for the payment of tuition fees. Even though undergraduate deferments are likely to be continued unless there is all-out mobilization, the change in policy from drafting the oldest first to drafting the youngest first will mean that far more and probably far abler young people will be applying for admission after they have completed their military service. As they approach the college gates, GI benefits in hand, the impact will be quite different on two kinds of institutions. At the public institution there will be less strain on the financial aid office, for most of the veterans' college expenses will be covered. But their presence will add immeasurably to the problem of finding enough space, unless academic and housing facilities are expanded more rapidly than they are being expanded at the present time. It may well be that a surge of veterans will lead to the necessity of tightening admissions standards for the high school graduating class.

For the high-cost private institution there will not be a surge of veterans unless the institution determines its willingness to devote additional financial aid in large amounts in order to make their attendance possible. Unless institutional financial aid resources expand more rapidly than they are doing at the present time, the private college admissions office is going to be faced with a dilemma. If it wishes to attract these mature and, as I predict, able and highly motivated students, it

24

may have to cut back sharply on its financial aid program for the high school graduating class.

All of this, of course, must be couched in speculative terms. No one can tell what, in terms of manpower or of years, our commitment may be in Vietnam. I doubt whether even the Pentagon can predict what the induction rate is likely to be as far ahead as next spring, let alone 1970. I do believe, however, that admissions officers must consider their policies toward veterans as an important element in their future operations. Since this colloquium is devoted to undergraduate policies, I shall not dwell on the topic from the point of view of the graduate school. I can only say that graduate deans should be even more concerned than undergraduate admissions officers with these questions.

I have, so far, been talking about a particular group of students who may be quite different from those admissions officers have customarily dealt with. But since 1958, and more intensively since 1965, the federal interest in higher education has been taking a shape that is profoundly affecting all admissions policies. So far, I suspect the impact has been minor and felt unevenly from institution to institution and from state to state.

I am referring to what I consider to be a determination in Washington that some form of higher, or postsecondary, education shall be available to all who aspire to it and can profit from it. Three times within the last two years President Johnson, in signing education bills, has proclaimed that now at last we can provide every boy and girl with "just as much education as he or she can take." This is, at the moment, confusing the dream with the reality. Even before the tragedy of Vietnam put severe strains on the federal budget, it was clear that the amount of money authorized was totally inadequate. Nevertheless, the dream is there, and it is not solely a Great Society dream. If partisanship again creeps into education legislation, and there are some signs that it may, the debate will probably be over means, not ends. There seems to be a firm commitment on the part of both parties to remove the financial barriers to higher education and throw the weight of federal resources, in any distinction that must be made between ability and need, on the side of need. Perhaps this comment is so obvious that it need not be made. But it has only become obvious since 1965, and prior to that time it was not at all clear whether the government would make any commitment to undergraduate students, beyond providing loans, and if it did, whether that commitment might not be to a massive kind of federal merit scholarship program.

25

The history of Title IV of the Higher Education Act of 1965 may be enlightening as a guide to future admissions policy. In 1961 President Kennedy's proposal to establish a federal scholarship program touched off a protracted, confused, and often bitter debate. There was the jurisdictional argument over the locus of administrative control, with sharp disagreement between those who favored institutional administration and those who insisted on state administration. There was a time when the difference seemed so irreconcilable that serious consideration was given to the possibility of federal administration.

There was adamant opposition in Congress to the concept that any young people should be given a "free ride" through college at government expense. This was shared equally by the most conservative elements and those bearing the label "liberal," who feared that scholarships would go to those least in need while the poor would have to continue to rely on loans. On the other side, there were those who believed that the government should put its weight behind quality, and there were serious proposals that a federal scholarship program should ignore entirely the concept of need.

The issues came to a head in 1962. The House stripped the higher education bill of any scholarship provision and sent to the Senate a bill that provided only for grants and loans for the construction of facilities. The Senate just as flatly, and overwhelmingly, wrote back into the bill the Kennedy scholarship proposal. Before the two bodies could go to conference to resolve their differences, the House Rules Committee extracted a promise from the House conferees that they would, under no circumstances, yield to the Senate on the matter of scholarships.

The Senate–House conferences were long, and stretched out over many weeks. The House conferees insisted, for reasons we need not go into here, that the Senate must yield on the issue of making grants, not contained in the Kennedy or Senate bills, to private (including church-related) institutions for academic facilities. When the Senate conferees acceded, the House had to find some way of making an important concession to the Senate, and the only issue left was scholarships.

By this time the National Defense Student Loan Program was in full operation and had been accorded by the Congress a degree of approval unusual for new educational ventures. The concept of financial need was deeply embedded—even fundamental—in the Act. At last, one inspired conferee suggested that the NDSL Program be expanded to provide "non-reimbursable loans" to students so needy that even under the generous terms of the basic loan program they could scarcely hope to

26

finance their college education. The concept was that they would borrow, with promise to repay, as much as they could from the basic loan program and then if this was not enough, they would be advanced a further "loan," which they need not repay, so that they might attend some college. All the Democratic conferees and, with the exception of the lame duck, then ranking member, all Republican conferees agreed to the proposal, including the Republican member who had previously bottled up the bill in the rules committee. Everyone concerned recognized the absurdity of the term "non-reimbursable loan"; everyone concerned recognized that it was a subterfuge to get around the mandate imposed by the rules committee. But more important, everyone concerned recognized that the bill would never have come out of conference if there had not been this concession.

The conference bill went to the floor of the House. The debate was again confused and bitter. The lame duck member led the attack on the conference report, charging with some justice that the House conferees had violated their pledge. The debate was compounded by a last-minute attack by the National Education Association on the constitutionality of the facilities grants program. The absurdity and confusion surrounding the debate is no better illustrated than by the fact that in the record there is a speech by Adam Clayton Powell, chairman of the House Committee on Education, attacking the conference report and indicating that he would vote against it. The speech had been drafted by his staff in his absence and inserted in the record at the appropriate point. The chairman himself appeared at the last minute and cast his vote in support of the conference report. Both the speech and the vote stand in the permanent record.

The NEA was given undue credit or blame, depending on one's point of view, for the defeat of the bill by a narrow 30-vote margin. A shift of 16 votes would have carried the day. I have always believed that it was the scholarship issue and the outrage of many House members that the House conferees had violated the spirit, if not the letter, of their commitment that lost the day.

The reason I have dwelled at such length on the defeated bill is that I believe that on that day in late September, at the end of a trying Congressional session when tempers were frayed, the patterns for the future were firmly drawn and that they will govern what colleges can and cannot, must and must not, do in the future if they are to work in tandem with the federal government. The Republican conferees who came back and supported the report, in spite of their embarrassment over the

27

term "non-reimbursable loan," are now the leaders on the minority side in the House. And what we now know as Educational Opportunity Grants are nothing more than "non-reimbursable loans" wearing a respectable suit of clothes.

This has an important implication for admissions policies in the future. As I interpret it, institutions and private foundations and even states are free to use their own resources as they see fit to reward merit, to continue tilling the rich suburban fields, to recruit where they wish to recruit and whom they wish to recruit. But if they choose to be participants in federal programs, they must commit themselves to going outside their normal ranges to till submarginal land, to make special concessions in their admissions and financial aid policies, and to devote their own resources to supplement federal funds in bringing about a real instead of a hypothetical equality of educational opportunity. I believe that the debate on what the major thrust of federal programs of student assistance was to be was settled in a hot smoky conference room in the Capitol, located exactly half way between the Senate and House chambers, one September afternoon in 1962. As is so often the case in the perspective of history, the issue was settled, despite a vote that temporarily rejected the compromises that had been reached.

Probably there are few institutions represented in this colloquium that can adhere strictly to their current admissions policies and still be major participants in the federal student aid programs as I see them developing. Perhaps there are institutions that can do a successful and important job and not commit themselves any more than they are now committed to the objectives of the government. But for most, a choice will have to be made, and I am not sure that dipping a tentative toe in the water, as most institutions have so far done, is going to be adequate. I think they are going to have to decide whether to sun themselves on a private beach or plunge themselves from a crowded strand into cold and choppy seas.

While I am discussing federal programs of student aid, it would be well to examine briefly one part of the Higher Education Act of 1965 that does not seem to fit the pattern I have described. I am referring to the Guaranteed Loan Program. So far this title has received remarkably little attention, even though potentially its effects can be revolutionary. As the program was enacted, it provided that students might borrow from $1,000–$1,500 per year through banks and other lending authorities. The states would set up mechanisms to administer the loans and provide, through state appropriations, a guarantee fund that would

28

protect the banks from loss. Maximum interest rate of 6 percent would be charged, and the federal government committed itself to paying the entire interest charge while the borrower was in college and all but 3 percent after he entered the repayment period.

The history of this legislation prior to enactment was interesting, and in that history there may be a clue to the direction the federal government will eventually go. The basic proposal was advanced by the Johnson Administration for two reasons. First, there was a growing conviction that some relief against increasing college expenses was needed for middle- and, as I see it, upper-middle-income families. But perhaps an even stronger motivation was the fear in the Treasury and in the Bureau of the Budget of the ultimate success of the many bills that had been introduced in both the Senate and the House to provide tax credits for payment of tuition, fees, and other educationally related expenses.

In 1964 the Administration had defeated by the narrowest of margins a drive in the Senate to enact a tax credit bill. It had used virtually all of its then impressive muscle on the Hill to switch the vote of several senators (including then Senator Humphrey) who had already committed themselves to sponsorship of the bill.

There are many who are puzzled by the bitterness of the Administration's fight against this measure. Yet I believe that it is likely to be opposed by any future Administration, whether Democratic or Republican, despite the commitment in the 1964 Republican platform to support it. Estimates of the cost of the program have varied considerably, largely because there has been no firm agreement on its precise provisions. But the bill introduced by Senator Ribicoff, now regarded as its chief spokesman, would, the Treasury believes, cost over $1.25 billion in its first year of operation and more in every subsequent year.

In a year when the country is spending nearly $5 billion on the space program, this does not seem a horrendous sum. But waiting in the wings are all sorts of other tax credit ideas. It would be a short step to move from providing tax credits for higher education to providing them for elementary and secondary education. It would also be a short step to providing tax credits for gifts made by taxpayers to educational institutions. Once the concept of granting credits to individual taxpayers is established—once a taxpayer is given the option of writing a check payable to a college or university (or some other eleemosynary enterprise) rather than to the Internal Revenue Service—there is every likelihood that there will be a steady erosion of the tax base,

29

with almost no control possible by either the appropriations committees of the Congress, or the Treasury and the Internal Revenue Service. I shall dwell briefly later on the pros and cons of the legislation from other points of view.

In any case, the Treasury was willing to go to almost any length to provide a politically acceptable substitute. The earliest drafts of the bill provided a straight guaranteed loan program at 6 percent interest with the federal government providing the guarantee. Later drafts provided a small interest subsidy—about 2 percent—while the borrower was a student, with the federal government providing the subsidy and the guarantee. Later the banking community, joined by other private interests, insisted that the bill should encourage the continuation and the establishment of state lending programs, and so responsibility for providing the guarantee was shifted to the states.

Still later the bill was changed, after some barometer reading on the Hill, to provide full interest payment by the government while the borrower was in college, and all but 3 percent after he graduated. The concept of need was entirely discarded except to eliminate the interest subsidy for families with incomes roughly above the $20,000 per year level.

For two reasons, the program, after almost two years, has yet to have any appreciable impact. Since the states were not consulted on their willingness to provide the guarantee funds, it is scarcely astonishing that they have shown little inclination to vote them. The impressive total of loans so far made—estimated to be $400 million—is accounted for largely by the fact that New York, with its previously existing and highly successful state program, is counted in the federal total, thanks to its having received temporary permission to continue its need requirement. The Congress had provided to the states a small amount of guaranty "seed money," eventually to be refunded to the Treasury, in order to enable the states and one private lending agency to make a start, but this seed money has virtually been exhausted.

A second important factor inhibiting the program's growth has been the steady rise since 1966 in the cost of money, and a consequent unwillingness or inability on the part of lending agencies to make money available, except on a token basis, at 6 percent.

There are now before the Congress Administration proposals that will unquestionably solve these problems. Although the banking community had been able almost to dictate the terms of the Act, it had, however reluctantly, agreed that if states proved unwilling to appropriate guarantee funds, the U.S. Commissioner of Education might move

30

in with a direct federal guarantee whenever he found that loans were not reasonably available to all eligible students. Before the next academic year begins, he is almost certain to exercise that authority. When he does, it seems reasonable to expect that even those states that have been moving toward providing state funds will reconsider. Furthermore, the federal guarantee will automatically add greatly to the sources of capital funds. For example, colleges themselves may well decide that the use of their own capital for these loans is a judicious and profitable investment. Investment opportunities involving no risk and yielding a return of 6 percent are not readily available to them.

Moreover, the Administration now proposes that the government shall pay all lending institutions a service charge of up to $35 for each loan put on the books and another service charge of up to $35 when a borrower's consolidated loans are put into the collection status. This device, rather than an increase in interest, has been adopted because of various state usury laws. It is impossible to compute the service fee device in terms of interest, because of variation in the size of loans, but it appears that the real return on these loans will be over 7 percent.

I have dwelt overlong on this program because I believe its implications are staggering and have not really been faced. If this program is the price of victory over tax credits, it may prove to be a Pyrrhic one.

Almost 90 percent of all college students and, indeed, most students in vocational education as well are eligible to borrow between $1,000–$1,500 per year and have the interest paid by the government. There are no built-in controls, for it is against the law to reject a loan because the borrower does not need it. If the loans are profitable, there will certainly be lending organizations ready to make them in almost limitless amounts. The Administration, in attempting to project the eventual cost of the program, seems to me to have adopted two totally invalid assumptions—that only a small percentage of the eligible borrowers will take advantage of the program and that they will borrow considerably less than the permissible maximum. I see no reason to suppose that any student, even if he has ample funds in the bank to pay for his education, will fail to take full advantage of the law. He is almost invited to do so. Why should he not leave his own funds in the bank earning 4 percent interest and borrow through the guarantee program at no cost to himself?

If my concerns are justified, the cost of this one program will put into serious jeopardy everything else the federal government is trying to do in the field of higher education. I greatly fear that with this

31

amount of easy money available the temptation for all institutions to raise their fees sharply will be irresistible, especially if the government finds that in order to finance the program, it must cut back its support for Educational Opportunity Grants, NDEA-type loans, facilities grants, graduate fellowships, and other programs that have been so painfully brought into being during the past 10 years. I believe that the admissions community, whose prime responsibility is the movement of a generation from secondary school into higher education, should be deeply concerned with all of this and should be studying its possible impact. As I see it, the instrument is already in being that can completely reverse the tradition that the older generation educate its young and instead place prime responsibility for payment upon the generation being educated. Perhaps this is the wave of the future, although I find myself hoping that it can be swept back. I do not, however, believe we should be drifting toward that wave apparently unaware that it is descending upon us.

If I may move now from the federal interest in student aid, I should like to consider the expressed federal interest in other areas that will inevitably have implications for admissions officers in the years to come. Some activities that in the past have seemed to be solely the concern of state and private nonprofit institutions are slowly being transferred to private profit-making enterprise. I am not at all sure that this is to be deplored, but I do believe we should know that it is happening. Obviously, we must, as a nation, invest increasing sums in subprofessional education and training. There is a conviction in Washington that unless we do, our whole economy will break down. Yet the history of higher education in these areas has not always been a happy one. It has proved itself unwilling or unable to police, through its system of accreditation, programs of such vital importance as medical technology. There is considerable doubt in my mind, for example, that it has offered as effective subprofessional technical programs as have been offered by the General Electric Company and the Radio Corporation of America on the one hand and the technical schools of the armed services and the Federal Aviation Agency on the other. I believe there is some evidence that job corps programs operated by industry have been far more effective than those administered by higher education. There is a proposed provision in Title IV of the Higher Education Act of 1965 to allow the Office of Education to contract with private enterprise for talent searching, rather than to rely solely on the often unimpressive efforts of higher education to search out this talent. I see a

32

dozen areas in which the pragmatist—and in the long run a Congressman must be pragmatic—might well decide that profit enterprise is better able to cope with some of the problems of the last third of the century than is our slow-moving system of higher education. If I may hark back, I believe President Johnson rightly expresses the interest of the federal government when he says that the country will assure every young person just as much education as he can take. But whether that education will be supported exclusively in our institutions of higher education depends on whether those institutions adapt themselves to the needs of the country. And now in conclusion I should like to move on to some of the thinking that is taking place in Washington on how we are to finance the mammoth enterprise we are committed to undertake.

The Vietnam War has put a freeze on the growth of current programs and has made unlikely the start of any new ones, except, perhaps, in a token way. It has not, however, led to any diminution of that favorite Washington pastime, the appointment of task forces to study the future. There are secret task forces, interagency task forces, intradepartmental task forces, coordinating committees, and planning groups. They have existed in the past, but for the most part they were oriented toward immediate action. Their mandate seemed almost to be, "Stop wasting your time thinking; propose something!"

Now, however, the very unlikelihood of immediate action may be leading to more rational analysis and solution. I'd like to sketch briefly the kinds of ideas that are being discussed. Some of them seem to me half-baked exercises in how to solve a problem without ever facing it. But that in itself is valuable, for it is easy to tell what is half-baked if there is enough time to chew on it and not swallow it whole.

There is still, as I have already discussed, the old proposal of providing tax credits for those who pay students' educational bills. For one brief moment recently, when Senator Long was trying to tie every lead weight he could find to sink a bill on the floor of the Senate, there was a vote by that body to enact a tax credit program. Everyone knew that the amendment would not survive this year, but the vote suggests that the proposal has life in it. Proponents argue that it will assist parents to pay for their children's education. They fail to note that it will do nothing for those most in need of help—youngsters from families too poor to pay taxes. The bewildering part of the proposal is the argument, simultaneously advanced, that it will aid institutions by enabling them to raise their fees and thus indirectly capture tax dollars without

33

pain to parents. Clearly, since these two so-called benefits are mutually exclusive, only one could prevail, and I would place my bet on an increase in fees. How could trustees of private institutions or state legislators decline such an invitation? The result would be the creation of an even greater gap between the pricing of higher education and the ability of hundreds of thousands of students to pay. We would obviously have to provide a massive increase in student aid programs, with all the expensive administrative machinery these programs inevitably entail.

A second proposal that is receiving serious discussion is that of returning federal tax funds to the states. The plan is generally ascribed to Walter Heller, former economic advisor to the President, and Joseph Pechman of The Brookings Institution, but there are as many variations on the theme as ever Paganini inspired. On the face of it, it is a simple plan to use the efficiency of the federal tax system to provide financial support to the states. The variations are largely those of delimitation—to allow or not to allow the funds to be used for highway construction; to require or not to require that the funds be used exclusively for education. My tentative judgment is that it makes very little difference whether or not the funds are earmarked. The cost to society of providing education will be so great that inevitably a large proportion of state revenues will go into it. If federally collected taxes are returned to the states, a large proportion must inevitably flow into the educational enterprise whether or not Congress directs that flow.

What concerns me is how the funds will be distributed within the states, and I am particularly concerned with the distribution of funds in higher education, which seems to me no longer to be a state or local concern. I happen to believe deeply in the diversity of higher education. I am not particularly concerned about the survival of church-related higher education as such, because that phrase seems to me to be more and more meaningless. Church-related higher education, except for the education of the religious orders, is becoming increasingly secular, and I am not at all sure that even today one could distinguish between the graduate of Notre Dame and the graduate of M.I.T. But I do deeply believe that the independence of private education is something that must be preserved, if only for the sake of public education. There are constant attacks on the autonomy of higher education from all directions. Public education has its John Birch Societies and the left wing critics to worry about. Private education has its unregenerate alumni and left wing pressure groups to worry about. But as long as

34

there is duality, our history suggests that pressures from extremists can be resisted.

If the tax-sharing concept should eventually become the prime vehicle for federal support of higher education, I fear that the duality of American higher education would be threatened. How would the funds be disbursed? If they were commingled with state funds and appropriated by the legislatures, we would have all of the problems now inherent in state-supported education without the anchor to windward of the private education system. Moreover, many state constitutions preclude the appropriation of state funds to support private education. If, on the other hand, the funds were turned over, without losing their federal identity, to a university grants commission within each state, the program could only further politicize an already too political process. There are states today in which such a program would work. But they would work largely because of the statesmanship of individuals who are more dedicated to the public weal than to private advancement. Remove those persons—those individuals—and replace them with other leaders chosen at random, and there could ensue a change from the comradeship of higher education to a match in which each party aimed for the jugular vein. I am inclined to think that the duality of higher education can survive only if there is a direct link between higher education and the federal government.

A third proposal is receiving an astonishing amount of attention in Washington these days. It was given prominence by President Kingman Brewster of Yale in a recent lecture at Stanford, although it has been around for a long time. The proposal is, again, a simple one. All institutions would raise their fees to approximately the cost of education. Students would then be allowed to borrow whatever they wished or needed to borrow in order to pay the cost. The loans would be repaid through a lifetime surtax on their federal income tax.

As far as I know, the proposal dates back to some ideas of Professor Seymour Harris of Harvard, who advanced them in the 1950s. It was his thesis that there is a dollar value that can be attached to higher education and that, therefore, heavy borrowing to secure it is a reasonable investment in an enterprise with assured growth potential. The proposal was later formally refined and enunciated by Professor Edward Shapiro in the Spring 1963 issue of the *Harvard Educational Review*.[1]

---

1. "Long-Term Student Loans: A Program for Repayment According to 'Ability to Pay,'" pp. 186-207.

The attraction of the plan is obvious. It is advanced as a way to pay for higher education without having to pay for it or, as I have suggested before, a way to solve a problem without really facing it. The basic proposition is that education is not an expense but an investment. The individual profits from his investment in education, and, therefore, he should be expected to pay for it. If he can, on the average, expect to earn one or two or three hundred thousand dollars more as a college graduate than he could have earned without a college education, then the surtax on his tax is a small price to pay.

There is an obvious catch in the proposal. What happens if the sheepskin does not turn into dollars? The answer is that on an actuarial basis the overpayment by those who strike it rich will counterbalance the underpayment by those who do not make out well financially and whose full borrowing, therefore, will never be repaid.

It would be presumptuous of me to be cavalier about a proposal that is receiving and perhaps should receive serious and prolonged study in places of power. Groups in the White House, the Treasury, the Bureau of the Budget, various nonprofit study centers, and even individual institutions are exploring the idea. At the moment one widely accepted estimate is that a charge of 1 percent of gross income for every $3,000 borrowed, paid over one's working lifetime, would make the program self-supporting. Those advocating the proposal thus point out that a loan of $15,000, roughly the cost of a college education, including some graduate work, today, would entail no more than a 5 percent tax on future income. What they seem to ignore is that, once the plan was adopted, the charge for a college education would inevitably rise and rise sharply. In fact, the proposal, like the Guaranteed Loan Program, invites such an increase.

In brief, I see the following objections to the proposal:

1. I believe an extraordinarily large percentage of college students know whether or not they are going to be financially well-to-do in their later careers. Those aiming for the ill-paid professions would opt for the program; those who saw the road ahead paved with gold would choose to borrow at high rates but at fixed terms rather than commit themselves to a lifetime of overpayment.

2. As far as I can see, there is no solution to the problem created by those who would borrow heavily but never enter the labor market. I am referring, of course, particularly to women, even though I know that a larger number of women are actually in the labor market for longer periods of time than ever before in history.

36

3. I believe the adoption of the proposal would bring about the end of voluntary support by individuals, by foundations, and by corporate enterprise for higher education. I would view this as an unmitigated tragedy.

To me the most promising discussions now taking place in Washington are directed toward helping institutions keep their charges down. In its simplest form this requires no more than a careful reexamination of existing programs. Institutions can, for example, build college housing through loans and pay the debt service through room rents. At present the government provides college housing loans at a flat 3 percent. If loans were provided interest free, there could be a reduction of approximately $200 in the annual room rent charged to students. If interest were to rise to 6 percent, which some groups favor, there would be a corresponding increase of $200 in annual room rent over current levels. It is my hope that in the near future it will be possible to determine which is the more economical direction. My guess is that expanding student aid programs for those who cannot pay existing or higher room rents is more expensive than providing the interest subsidy. Every existing federal program must be analyzed with similar alternatives in view, whether they are for research support; facilities construction; curriculum reform; purchase of equipment; extension, vocational, and adult education; or urban renewal.

But beyond this reappraisal, I believe we are moving to more general federal support of the total higher education enterprise. This will present enormous problems. Should it be on a strict formula base—so many dollars per head with perhaps some variation allowed for the obvious difference in cost between educating a freshman and educating a doctoral candidate?

The problem with the formula grant is that it goes equally to the best and the worst of our institutions. There are many who believe that the whole nation would profit if many of our existing institutions were allowed to perish. We know that there are medical schools so bad that most of us would not willingly submit ourselves to the care of their graduates. We know that there are undergraduate colleges whose graduates can barely read and write—and unfortunately many of them will be teaching the next generation. In Title III of the Higher Education Act of 1965, the so-called developing-institutions title, we have made a timid start in tackling this problem. We have said in effect that these institutions exist, that they are going to have students, and that what they produce will, for good or ill, affect all of society. And so we have voted to provide them with funds—knowing that money alone will not improve them, but knowing even better that without money they cannot improve.

But the debate is not over. Many in Congress who have supported the measure seriously doubt whether their support is wise. Might it not be better to follow the dictum of the traffic expert who, confronted by history's most monumental traffic jam, recommended that we pave over the tops of the cars and start again from scratch? My own guess is that major support of higher education through formula grants will be possible only if we develop a better basis for determining quality. In our lifetime this will be a task left to higher education itself. We are not ready yet, if indeed we ever will be, for governmental determination of standards.

Yet as I say that, I know that in a sense I am contradicting existing patterns. In the area of science we are already providing general support to institutions on the basis of their existing or their potential quality. The National Science Foundation believes that it is possible to identify institutions that, with the infusion of large grants of federal funds over a period of several years, can be brought from adequacy to greatness. It is committing considerable sums to this belief. Before making a grant, it requires evidence of imaginative leadership, thoughtful planning, potential long-term support, and a sustained commitment to intellectual excellence. Those who are fearful that formula support will perpetuate mediocrity point to the NSF programs as the proper alternative.

But, argue the opponents, if this is the wave of the future, who is to play God? If the NSF kind of thinking had prevailed in 1862, we would never have had our great system of land grant colleges. No one would have known how to write a proposal; there was no Washington secretariat skilled in the art of grantsmanship; nowhere available was the faculty and administrative staff to provide the panels to judge the proposals to fund the projects to support their own institutions. In short, there are many today who believe that our whole proposal–project system, which requires individual and often subjective judgment, has already gone too far. There is fear that unless we turn back toward placing more responsibility in institutions as institutions and let them develop their own innovations, set their own priorities, and work out their own patterns, the whole structure of higher education will break down.

I am certain that general federal support for higher education lies down the road. I am not at all certain which basic view will prevail, but it is reasonable to suppose that, as is almost always the case in our society, there will be a compromise—a certain amount in formula grants with an additional amount reserved for incentive grants, support of innovational projects, and development awards to carry out specific projects of interest to individual institutions.

I come now to the end, not because the topic but because the reader must be exhausted. The federal interest in higher education and its probable involvement in the lives and work of admissions officers are potentially limitless. I have barely skimmed the surface and could easily do an entire book on the subject. It seems clear to me, however, that whatever the picture an institution is trying to draw of itself, be it a small liberal arts college or a giant public university, it will find itself a part of a mosaic that the nation, working through its elected officials in Washington, is creating. It can create a part of that mosaic and help shape the way the rest is drawn. But the tide is running strong to force all institutions to be responsive and relevant to the nation's needs. Those that cannot or will not fit the picture will disappear or will be hung in the portrait gallery as reminders of past splendor.

State Plans for Higher Education and Their Influence on Admissions

Charles W. Sanford

The major interest of the state in higher education that will affect college admissions policies in the decade ahead might be stated as follows:

"The opportunity to study in institutions of higher education should be available to all young people who may reasonably be expected to benefit from such study. . . . Society suffers a substantial loss because many qualified young people do not now enroll in colleges and universities and many others drop out of college before completing degree or certificate programs. . . . Able students who could not otherwise attend institutions of higher learning should have the opportunity to qualify for financial assistance from institutional sources or from the state or nation. . . . Because of the expanding need for persons with professional and technical skills, and the continuing need for general (liberal) education for all citizens, the State should plan for a larger proportion of youth to attend colleges and universities than is now the case. . . . It is desirable that the principle of free choice by the student among the various institutions, large or small, public or non-public, be maintained so far as consistent with admissions policies and effective use of resources within the State. . . . Substantial benefit to the State will result from expanded programs of adult and specialized education."[1]

This major interest or goal of the state must be rooted in statewide understanding and acceptance, which in turn necessitates statewide planning, organization, and action. And successful planning, organization, and action must involve a systematic recognition of many other important interests. The interests include—to mention a number—those of students, parents and other laymen, representatives of state government, state boards of higher education, institutional boards of trustees, the faculties of institutions of higher learning, the faculties of public and private high schools, and accrediting agencies.

An analysis of these interests reveals problems related to the number and the quality of the students to be educated, the number and the quality of the faculties needed, the nature of the educational programs to be offered, the organization of the institutions to be encouraged, the

---

1. *A Master Plan for Higher Education in Illinois*, Illinois Board of Higher Education, July, 1964, pp. 6-7.

40

extent and type of physical facilities needed, and the finances required. I will consider primarily the problem of the number and the quality of the students to be educated.

State interests affecting college admissions policies in the next decade will, then, focus on students and what they need in higher education to make the state the kind of state the people want, on the students and what they need to make them the kind of citizens they want to be and the state wants, and on ways and means of accomplishing both by developing and financing the program needed.

The answer to the question of the number of students who are to obtain postsecondary education has been proposed—that all qualified youth, all who have completed secondary school, should have opportunities available to them in postsecondary institutions in each state. The welfare of the state and of its citizens can dictate no less.

This quantitative goal for the state should be achieved for all students in some institution, public or private, two-year or four-year, technical or semitechnical. Hence, the opportunities for achieving this goal must be assessed—and reassessed periodically—by reviewing the total picture of all institutions in a state.

Magnitude of the quantitative goal. One illustration of the magnitude of the quantitative problem may be apropos. It is recognized that most high schools are offering preparation for colleges and universities that is far superior to that which was offered 35 or 40 years ago. All the evidence indicates that this is true. Moreover, the high schools have made excellent progress in refining the assessment of students' capabilities and interests to the end that those who should attend college are encouraged to do so, and that those who should participate in another form of postsecondary education are encouraged to do so. And colleges and universities have, I am sure, also improved their programs for the assessing of students' capabilities and interests and for counseling.

Nevertheless, the national and state pictures reveal that the country must accomplish a great deal to make the quantitative goal a reality. In Illinois, for example, the *Master Plan for Higher Education* indicates that 25 percent of the students in the state in the top quarter of their high school graduating classes and 44 percent in the second quarter do not go on to college. I strongly support the conclusion cited that "This evidence indicates that Illinois has much to do in encouraging high-ability students to enter college."[2]

---

2. *Ibid.*, p. 24.

41

Need for accurate quantitative data. Given this quantitative goal, each state is faced with the determination of the number of students involved and costs. During the next decade, representative admissions officials should serve as advisory committees to the staffs of state planning bodies and collaborate with them in taking whatever steps are necessary to provide accurate projections of the numbers involved by types of institutions, by sex, and by class level. The admissions officials should provide expertise that will lead to such precision that accurate data will be available for planning and that the accuracy, in turn, will result in the acceptance of the projections by state governments and laymen.

Now I will turn to the question of the quality of the students to be admitted. While all qualified students who wish to have opportunities available to them should be admitted, it does not follow that a given student should be admitted to any institution, or that all will wish to attend some type of institution. It does follow that a given qualified student should be admitted to some institution and that the states need to examine carefully the reasons for a lack of interest in postsecondary education on the part of some students.

Problems related to the quality of the students to be admitted. As a state plans for the quality of the students who will be admitted to its colleges, it is confronted with an interesting array of problems related to the desired distribution of student talent of various types among institutions, the extent to which institutions are in a position to offer programs that meet the needs of students with particular qualifications, the relationship between the socioeconomic status of students and the expenses of attending certain institutions, the wishes of institutions with regard to the nonintellective characteristics sought in the student body, the mix of students wanted from other states and nations, the commitment of various institutions within the state to experimentation in admissions such as through the admission of a certain number of "gamble" cases, and numerous other problems that any admissions officer could identify. Each of these problems involves state interests that affect the colleges' admissions policies but over which the state has—and doubtless should continue to have—varying degrees of influence and control.

Admissions processing center and data bank. In each state, in the decade ahead, increasingly accurate data should be obtained, through sophisticated procedures, for reaching decisions concerning students' qualifications and their admission to various types of institutions. An

42

admissions processing center and data bank should be organized in each state to provide the basic information that every public institution needs to determine the qualifications of applicants, including as a minimum, high school percentile rank, test scores, and the records of past successes of students from High School X or College Y in College A. Perhaps private institutions will wish to use this center. We hope they will. Participating public and private institutions may want supplementary data that they can obtain independently of the center. The processing center and data bank, administered by the state agency in charge of statewide planning, should provide a level of expertise and data to institutions that could not otherwise afford them, and it would enable the state to obtain an accurate picture, in terms of common definitions, for the entire state. The potential of such a statewide center and bank go far beyond the values indicated. The important point is that each institution would have available the most accurate data that statistical procedures and good machines can produce for use in making judgments concerning the students to be admitted to a given institution. And the state, through its agency for viewing statewide provisions and needs, would have accurate and reliable statewide data for its uses.

Data on student characteristics. A wealth of data are now being made available on student characteristics by such studies as the one initiated in the fall of 1966 by the American Council on Education, which involved a survey of entering freshmen, and the SCOPE study (School to College: Opportunities for Postsecondary Education), sponsored by the College Entrance Examination Board and devoted to student decision making and its outcomes.

During the next decade, selected features of these and other studies should be incorporated into statewide data banks. The data should prove to be extremely helpful in determining the extent to which a given state is meeting its obligation in the provision of postsecondary education. They should also help students and their counselors and parents to determine the type of curriculum and institution that the students should enter. Pertinent statewide data should, in turn, be incorporated into other data banks that seem to offer promise, such as the National Research Bank of the American Council on Education. The opportunities are many for extremely significant long-range research and for various types of longitudinal studies on both a state and a national basis.

Articulation programs and the quality of the students admitted. In

43

the immediate years ahead, institutional and statewide programs of school and college articulation should become precise to the point that students may move from one institution to another in smooth transition. The base for such programs must be a body of data concerned with the performance of students from a given high school or college in a given institution to which they transfer.

One example may be apropos. The Illinois Council on Articulation, a statewide body representative of all private and public institutions in Illinois, approved in June 1967 a study "to determine the performance of transfer students in Illinois institutions of higher education. An analysis of the problem results in the following questions which need to be studied:

"1. What is the magnitude of the transfer population in Illinois educational institutions?

"2. What are the mobility patterns of transfer students between institutions?

"3. What are the intellectual and academic characteristics of students who transfer to the various types of institutions?

"4. How successful are transfer students in the achievement of their stated academic goals after transfer? . . ."[3]

The design of the study involves ". . . a survey of the mobility and performance of transfer students in Illinois institutions of higher education. There is no attempt in this study to manipulate variables or change conditions which may affect the performance of transfer students. . . . It is proposed that all students who transfer during the 1967-68 academic year (Fall, Winter, and Spring terms) be included in the sample for the proposed study. The study should include all of the institutions of higher education in Illinois who either send or receive transfer students." It is heartening to note the cooperation of all segments of higher education, public and private, two-year and four-year, in tackling a problem of this type.

Strong institutional articulation programs will require extensive counseling of students both before and after transfer and the provision of information and data to the counselors in the schools from which they wish to transfer. It will also involve an exchange of information among institutions to achieve a high order of coordination in subject-matter content and in counseling activities.

---

3. "Proposal for a Study of the Performance of Transfer Students," p. 3. Mimeographed.

44

What is the role of admissions officers in assisting a student in getting into the college that would seem to be best for him? All of us would doubtless agree that, with very few exceptions, there is no one college that is best for a particular student. There are probably a large number of institutions that would be quite satisfactory and equal in helpfulness to this given student. But after this has been said, it must be recognized that a student cannot obtain a program in forestry if a given college does not offer a program in forestry, and that a student who is mediocre in academic abilities should not be admitted to an institution in which 98 percent of the students rank in the top 5 percent in academic abilities. Moreover, the expenses restrict the choices of college for many students. The restriction has fortunately been reduced somewhat by the addition of such sources of financial aid as state scholarship programs, and the federal Educational Opportunity Grants Program.

The admissions officer is, then, confronted with the necessity for developing a very strong program of articulation with the secondary schools and with other colleges from which students transfer to his institution. This program of articulation should help administrators, counselors, and teachers in high schools and in colleges to understand the types of students who should do well in the institution to which they wish to transfer. This understanding cannot be developed unless the institution to which they wish to transfer has defined its purposes in terms that can be used in admissions criteria, and this can only happen when continuous research has been conducted, year after year, to validate the criteria used. Moreover, the research must include the success of students from the individual high schools and colleges concerned.

At the statewide level, instruments should be adapted or adopted such as the *Guidelines for Improving Articulation Between Junior and Senior Colleges*, a statement by the Joint Committee on Junior and Senior Colleges of the Association of American Colleges, the American Association of Junior Colleges, and the American Association of Collegiate Registrars and Admissions Officers.[4] Such guidelines are extremely helpful in the implementation of a strong program that involves a large number of different types of colleges and universities.

The admission of nonresident students and the denial of qualified resident students. The relationship between the quality of the students admitted and the number and percentage of nonresident students admitted becomes acute when qualified resident students are denied ad-

---

4. American Council on Education, 17 pp.

mission even though the nonresident students have superior qualifications. Ideally, we should dispense with state lines and eliminate higher tuition and fees and higher admissions requirements for applicants from other states and countries. Practically, I suspect that this would require some form of national action at a very high level. I would hope that steps could be taken during the next decade that would lead to such action.

Academic communities place a high premium on diversity of population. Opportunities for contacts with students from different states and nations should be provided for all students in a given university. The federal government is participating very heavily in the financing of selected activities in various universities, and it follows that each institution has some obligation, although one is not imposed, to consider carefully the scope of its nonresident attendance within the context of national and state interests.

The problem of the number and percentage of nonresident students to be accepted varies in some institutions at the undergraduate and graduate levels. Graduate and professional students are considered in many institutions as personnel who are needed for both teaching and research. Without a national market in graduate enrollment, it would be difficult for many universities to maintain a strong graduate college and continue to produce the large numbers of teachers and other professional people whom business and educational institutions need.

Nevertheless, public institutions in a number of states have been asked either to hold the line or to curtail the percentage of nonresident or foreign students, or both, admitted. During the next decade, this problem should be solved, or at least minimized, by establishing provisions that will encourage student mobility. The provisions should dispense with state line restrictions, they should provide for the payment to institutions of the per capita cost of foreign students, and they should specify some desired number of foreign students to be admitted to each institution and to the country as a whole. Obviously, each institution will need to specify the number of foreign students to be admitted, and the total for all institutions should be in terms of national goals with regard to international understanding and progress.

Obligation to assist the "under-educated" but able student. The *Master Plan* for Illinois recommends that "The junior colleges develop and experiment with programs especially designed to aid the under-educated student of post-high school age to prepare as speedily as possible for transfer to senior institutions at the junior level or for entry directly

46

into employment from technical and semi-technical programs."[5] No doubt others have wondered, as I have, why so many students shun college. I entertain the hope that junior colleges will achieve ever-increasing success in enrolling and then in raising the aspirations of students who possess the ability for college-level work, but presently bypass college. Junior colleges are in an excellent position to identify and assist students who have matured more slowly than their peers, students who are economically disadvantaged, and students who possess correctable deficiencies. A considerable number of these students now find it impossible to meet the admissions requirements of many four-year colleges. Given a year or two of additional time, special counseling, and remedial work, many of them would be in a position to proceed successfully in a four-year institution. Others would take occupational-oriented programs and be prepared on graduation to be employed.

As institutions of higher learning become parts of statewide systems of higher learning, they move into different arenas of operation. In the admission of students, increased precision is required in public institutions in validating admissions requirements, in projecting enrollments, in establishing quotas, and in registering the specified number and types of students. Moreover, increased attention must be given to the admissions problems of other public institutions and of private colleges and universities. These are essential elements in state planning.

For instance, at Institution A, we can admit students to Curriculum 1 in Institution A from High School X or College Y in terms of any predicted degree of success we wish to use, within the limits of the accuracy of our measures of prediction. But to do so, we must build up data on the relationship between the success of students from High School X or College Y in Curriculum 1 in Institution A. In addition, we must know, in statewide planning, the exact number of students we want in Curriculum 1.

The predicted degree of success that is used in admissions becomes extremely important when the planning stipulates quotas of students, and dollars and cents are attached to each student that the institution registers. Thus, an institution might have a quota of 6,000 beginning freshmen, 200 of whom are to be admitted to Curriculum 1. If the state formula stipulates the institution is to receive $1,000 per student from the state for each beginning freshman and sophomore registered, $1,500 for each junior and senior, $2,000 for each beginning graduate

---

5. *Op. cit.*, p. 35.

47

student, and $4,500 for each advanced graduate student, it is obvious that a high order of precision must obtain in the number of students registered at each level. And if the instructional facilities in Curriculum 1 for beginning freshmen are limited to 200, it is obviously not possible to exceed this number. Moreover, if the budget plan in a state provides for penalties for under- or over-enrollments, the admissions officer is confronted with the additional need for accuracy and precision. Since budgets are planned far in advance, often two years ahead of enrollments, and since some institutions are enrolling 45,000 or 50,000 students, it becomes essential to work out ways and means in the next decade for adjusting the relationship between enrollments and budgets in such a way that the realities of the enrollment situation will be recognized without the gain or loss of large sums of money to the institutions concerned. It is conceivable that conditions with regard to enrollments can change between the time the budget is prepared and actual registration in such a way that an institution is rewarded dollarwise for overprojecting and underenrolling.

The realities of the enrollment situation indicate that state planners must be able to know that student spaces will be available, and this means that institutional planners must designate the number of students they will accept. To enroll accurately the number designated, when an enrollment of 45,000 or 50,000 students is involved, and to do so two years in advance by class level, and by college or curriculum or both, necessitates the establishment of realistic quotas and the determination of percentages of leeway that will be permitted. Good institutional and statewide procedure will, it is proposed, provide a 3-percent leeway in total enrollment, up and down, and reimbursement for both. Thus, an institution would receive reimbursement for each student up to 3 percent above the total quota and would return reimbursement when the enrollment was more than 3 percent below the total. The procedure would also permit the institution to make adjustments among class levels.

To return to the example of 200 freshmen to be admitted to Curriculum 1, it is not difficult to work out tables of predicted grade-point averages and also tables that indicate the success of students from given high schools. After the tables have been prepared and the applications for admission examined, we might say that no students will be invited to attend unless they have a predicted grade-point average of 4.0 or B. The problem, and it is a real problem both statewide and nationwide, is when an institution should issue the permit to enter. All

48

institutions of higher learning are presently having difficulties with this point since so many practices obtain with regard to notification dates. If an institution waits until April 1 or May 1 to issue permits for the following September, it is apt to lose a considerable number of highly qualified students because of the students' anxiety to be admitted and their having had offers from other institutions. If the institution uses two or three notification dates, it may find itself in the position of filling Curriculum 1 with 4.0 and 4.1 students on the first or the first and second notification dates and thus having to deny 4.5 and 4.6 students later on, in April or May. This problem points to the desirability of establishing on the state level, but preferably on the national level, one or at the most two announcement dates that would be followed by all institutions. This would be of inestimable help to the students who are applying for admission and also to the institutions that they wish to enter.

The recognition of these and other state interests affecting admissions policies requires an extremely high order of cooperation and of coordination among secondary schools and institutions of higher learning.

Each institution of higher learning places a high premium on varying degrees of autonomy. The preservation of this autonomy in a statewide system with clearly defined statewide goals is indeed difficult. There is always the possibility that the statewide planners will usurp the prerogatives of institutional planners. While this possibility is real, the premium placed on the goals sought through statewide planning and organization causes institutions to risk the possibility. As they take this calculated risk, statewide and institutional planners collaborate in defining lines of responsibility and of governance that will lead to the desired balance in institutional autonomy and statewide organization.

In admissions there seems to be a contradiction. The contradiction is rooted in the similarity of admissions requirements and the dissimilarity of programs.

Some colleges and universities admit the number of beginning freshmen they want by selecting those with the highest high school percentile rank or grade-point average. Other institutions consider tests scores in some manner. Still other institutions prescribe the completion of certain high school subjects. Others consider recommendations from the high school. And there are still others that combine two or more of these and add others. The problem develops when the admissions variables used fail to measure the competencies needed for successful work in the curriculum the student wishes to enter. During the next decade, it is anticipated that marked gains will be recorded in specifying the competencies needed for successful work in each of the many curriculums offered in institutions of higher learning and in the refinement of the variables employed in admissions. The refinement of these variables necessitates extensive experimentation on new and imaginative admissions models.

The junior colleges seem to be in a fortunate position with regard to this phase of admissions in that they admit all high school graduates and then apply a wide variety of subjective and objective evaluations to help a student obtain the program that best matches his interests and abilities.

These factors, and others, point to the need in statewide planning for recognizing the mission and stated functions of each institution, private and public. A comprehensive statewide program must consider each institution, though legal governance is, of course, limited to the public.

I close on the cheerful note that the achievement of such state interests affecting admissions policies as have been cited will necessitate the further professionalization of the admissions office. The necessity for leadership from this office is clear. Admissions officials must deal, in an increasingly sophisticated manner, with admissions, relations with high schools and colleges, testing and research, student data systems, and financial aids. The consideration of policy and procedural questions concerned with each of these functions must include recognition of the integral relationship of these functions within an institution and within the state and nation. And this means that admissions offices must be staffed to do this job.

Being staffed to do the job refers to the numbers of staff members needed and the quality and educational training of the professional personnel.

The admissions office has a service function to perform. It also has an important leadership function. It has a significant role in academic planning in the institution in terms of the philosophy and purposes of the institution. Therefore, the office of admissions must be staffed with persons with strong academic and research backgrounds. Most institutions of higher learning will welcome the kind of leadership that offices of admissions can render if these offices are indeed academically oriented and understanding of the problems of all divisions of the institution.

This will come about only if admissions officers offer the kind of

50

leadership that attracts and merits the confidence of the university administration and the academic divisions. This challenge in the next decade rests with those in admissions who hold these positions of leadership.

51

Clear Institutional Objectives
Essential to Admissions Function

John D. Millett

In a time of a shortage of goods and an excess of demand, it is a popular procedure to find fault with someone. In the case of college admissions, it is frequently the lot of the admissions officer to catch the brickbats. If an individual high school applicant is successful in gaining admission to the college of his or her first or second choice, the credit goes entirely to the applicant for his or her outstanding achievement, which could not be denied this appropriate recognition. If an individual high school applicant is unsuccessful in gaining admission to the college of his or her first or second choice, the blame falls upon the admissions officer who obviously can't recognize a meritorious admissions application when he sees one.

It is my impression from meeting and knowing a great many admissions officers that they do a very good job under difficult circumstances. The admissions officer in a college that practices selective admissions because of limited facilities and resources or because of limited instructional objectives is expected to exercise judgment and to accept only those students who best fit the program or programs of the institution he serves. This is a necessary function indeed and one whose importance and delicacy seldom receive the appreciation they deserve.

While I thus acknowledge the special contribution made to institutions of higher education by the admissions officers, I must nonetheless find some fault with the way the admissions function is handled. Let me make this distinction clear. The admissions officer is not the object of my concern. The admissions function is. And my concern arises from a conviction that the deficiencies in the admissions function cannot be corrected by admissions officers.

In spite of all the discussion in recent years about the importance of educational objectives in determining the peculiar role and practice of each individual college or university, I am inclined to believe that institutions of higher education have not taken this injunction as seriously as they might. And part of the failure arises from the lack of a clear understanding about the choices that confront each institution of higher education.

It follows, I believe, that if educational objectives are not clearly formulated and explicitly stated, then the selection of students for admission to a college or university will tend to be confused and confusing. Indeed, I think that a very good part of the criticism that confronts admissions officers today might be dissipated if the educational objectives of an institution were more clearly defined. I have no illusions that all difficulties could be eliminated, but I would like to see the effort made to clarify admissions selections in relation to educational objectives.

Actually, I see no good reason why a particular college or university might not go farther. After all, the action of applying for admission is a voluntary one on the part of an individual prospective student. As a part of such action, I think an institution might inquire about the extent of the understanding of and commitment to these objectives on the part of the applicant and the applicant's family as one factor in the selection process. When a student is admitted to an institution, he and his family should clearly understand not only the financial obligations they are assuming but also the educational obligations they are assuming.

I want to emphasize here that I am talking about undergraduate education for the baccalaureate only. I am not interested here in graduate or graduate professional education, or admission thereto. I am considering only the various undergraduate curriculums to which a high school graduate may seek access. I would emphasize also that applicants and institutions need to have a meeting of the minds *during* the admissions process. Afterwards, it is too late. The institution is stuck with the student, and the student is stuck with the institution. The relationship can be an unhappy one or a satisfactory one. Whether the relationship is one or the other depends in major part, I believe, upon how well the admissions function is performed. And this functioning in turn, I submit, depends upon how well the educational objectives of an institution are explained in advance of admission, and how well the interests of the institution and the interests of the student are interwoven in the selection process.

Let me add a footnote here. I wish institutions could get beyond the stage where admission is thought of primarily in terms of test scores on a scholastic aptitude or scholastic achievement test. Scholastic aptitude and scholastic achievement are only two of several factors that are and necessarily must be involved in any student selection procedure for college admission. There are other factors involved as well, and all factors should contribute to the decision on whether a prospec-

53

tive student's total abilities, interests, and inclinations fit the educational objectives of an institution. Colleges need to select students not upon the basis of scholastic aptitude but upon the basis of institutional aptitude, upon the basis of a student's relationship to the educational objectives of an institution.

As I have analyzed this matter of educational objectives, I have come to the conclusion that three pairs of basic choices confront every institution in defining its basic purpose and confront every prospective student in deciding where to apply for an undergraduate education. These choices are:

1. Residential education versus urban education.
2. General education versus professional education.
3. Supervised education versus independent education.

There may be other choices as well, but these are the essential ones. I recognize there is nothing new in this array of choices insofar as educational objectives are concerned. I only wish institutions were more forthright in their avowal of purpose and more insistent in their dedication of effort for the fulfillment of their avowed purposes. As in so many other walks of American life, the colleges and universities are likely to try to be all things to all people.

The original colonial conception of a college in America was copied from Oxford and Cambridge universities in England. In the colonies with their sparse and widely scattered population no other arrangement would have been feasible in any event. We did not become an urban nation until this century. The prototype of the colonial and of the nineteenth-century college in America was a residential college where students lived in dormitories on a campus, usually in a small town. To many persons the idea of a college is still the residential institution, even though 70 percent of all Americans now live in urban centers and even though in some instances the residential college or university now is surrounded by a bustling, teeming city.

The urban college or university is a phenomenon of twentieth-century America. The urban college or university finds its educational mission in the urban environment of which it is an integral part. The undergraduate and graduate students are preponderantly residents of the urban area. Many of these students are part-time students, working while seeking an education or wanting education as a supplement to their employment. The urban college or university serves primarily commuting students. The urban college or university usually is heavily involved in the public service effort of continuing professional educa-

54

tion, because professional practitioners are heavily concentrated in the cities.

One reason—I believe it to be the most important reason—that the junior or community college has flourished in this country in the past 45 years is because this college was specifically oriented to urban America. The higher education system in this country was slow to recognize or to accommodate itself to the rapid urbanization of American society. As a result, the community college, which was devised particularly to serve urban communities, had a unique opportunity for educational service. The community college was quick to take advantage of this opportunity.

There are several obvious differences between the residential and the urban college. The most important difference is readily apparent. The student at a residential college lives his entire life in the college community. The student at an urban college lives part of his life, the instructional part, in the college community and the other part of his life in the urban community. In the residential college, the institution must provide living quarters for the student, or usually must provide some supervision of living quarters. The residential college must be concerned about the health, the recreational, and the social conditions of student life. What should be the degree of this concern I shall consider later. But the concern itself cannot be eliminated from the residential college by the very nature of its residential characteristic.

Ordinarily, in the urban college matters of students' health, recreation, and social activity fall upon the urban community as a whole and not upon the academic community. To be sure, the urban college may find it desirable to maintain a student center facility, to publish a student newspaper, to organize or promote occasional social activities such as student dances. But the urban college expects the urban community to absorb much of the student's life—all of that life spent off-campus.

I wish I could say that the urban college alone has the distinctive characteristic of providing acres of parking space for its commuting students. But, unless the residential college makes it a condition of student residential life to prohibit the use of automobiles, the residential campus will be equally inundated today with automobiles. Indeed, the parking situation may be even worse at the residential college because the automobiles are there all day and all night, except generally on weekends.

In the past, many claims have been made for the educational supe-

55

riority of the residential college. The student living with other students was expected to advance his education by the continual contact with other students. To be sure, in a tutorial system of instruction, a close integration of residence and education was the essence of the procedure. Even where the tutorial system of instruction as such did not exist, the residential college nonetheless was supposed to promote or encourage a close social relationship between students and faculty. In fact, there is some question whether students see any more of faculty members on a residential campus than on an urban campus.

Today, educational realists would question just how much education is actually achieved within a full-time student society. If the process of peer group interaction is to be labeled education, it is assuredly a type or kind of education that is not duplicated in the classroom. The residential college does tend to bring together in subgroupings students of like interest and to promote organizational activity in which students acquire some capacities for social endeavor, or togetherness. The residential college at the same time may actually be an unfortunate or unrealistic social environment, because outside the college the student will find a greater range of ages and a greater range of social conflict than usually occurs among student groups.

The residential college may be important as a part of the process of student emotional and individual maturation. The really important aspect of the residential college is the opportunity it affords the student to live away from the protective and perhaps the inhibiting circumstances of family life. The conditions of family life are perhaps so varied today that no generalization can really be made about the circumstances from which students seek to escape. And undoubtedly parents are often as eager to send their sons and daughters away from home as the sons and daughters are to leave home. The motivation in both cases can scarcely be labeled educational in any strict definition of that word. The residential college is thus expected to pursue its instructional objectives within a social environment where the student is as much concerned with his freedom from parental supervision as he is with his intellectual growth.

Certainly, there are family circumstances in modern urban life that are anything but conducive to educational achievement by the student. If a family has no educational tradition, no respect for or understanding of the importance of education, and no willingness to accept the current income loss of education, then the individual member of the family pursuing an educational program labors under a major handi-

56

cap. Such a person is better off to leave the family and pursue his own line of interest, including, it is to be hoped, an educational goal. It is important to observe, however, that the prospective student from a family hostile to education is seldom able to find his way to a residential college either. He is more apt to find employment and an education in an urban setting.

It must be remembered that the residential college is much more expensive for an individual student to attend than the urban college. The residential college must charge the student not only for instruction but also for room and board, as well as for student health and social services. If the residential college is privately sponsored, it will have some endowment and gift income to subsidize instructional expense. If the residential college is publicly sponsored, it will have some tax income to subsidize instructional expense. But both the privately and publicly sponsored residential college must expect the student or his family to pay the full cost of room and board and other special student residential services.

Moreover, the residential college must worry about finding the funds for the capital facilities of a residential campus, while the urban college can concentrate its concern upon the capital facilities needed for instruction. This situation makes the residential college much more expensive to finance insofar as capital plant is concerned. And these capital plant costs include not only residential facilities as such but also the sidewalks, streets, lawns, playgrounds, water supply, sewage disposal, lighting, and other required utilities.

The first major choice accordingly that faces an institution is whether it is going to be residential in character or urban in its orientation. The first major choice that confronts the student is whether he is going to seek to attend the residential or the urban college. Incidentally, because of cost and size limitations, it is the residential college that is usually more selective in its admission. It is usually easier for the student to gain access to the urban institution whose objective is to provide educational opportunity to persons living in the urban community.

In the second place, at the undergraduate level of instruction there is a choice to be made between general education and professional education as the objective of a baccalaureate program. I wish that the labels or definitions were more adequate to express the contrast, or the different purposes, that I have in mind here. The prevailing practice in this country is still to speak of a liberal education at the undergraduate

57

level, or of education in the liberal arts, as against professional education that culminates in a baccalaureate.

In fact, there is no such thing in this country as a clear, precise definition of liberal education. This situation is readily evident from Daniel Bell's study, *The Reforming of General Education*, published in 1966.[1] The American college as it existed up until the Civil War did have a fairly standard curriculum based on the classic languages and literature of Greek and Latin, history and political economy, mathematics, philosophy and theology, and so-called natural philosophy. This standard course of study was considered as the desirable collegiate preparation for the two major professions of the day, the ministry and the law. I once reviewed the professional careers of the 1,000 graduates of Miami University in the period between 1826 and 1873. I found that one-third of these graduates had become ministers, one-third lawyers, and the remaining one-third had entered a wide variety of occupations including medicine, business, college teaching, and public service.

After the Civil War, a greater variety of professions began to emerge in the United States and a corresponding variety of undergraduate professional education programs began to appear. Today there is a considerable range of undergraduate professional education programs that the college student may pursue for four and occasionally five years after high school graduation. These include: education for elementary or secondary school teaching, business administration, engineering, architecture, art, music, nursing, agriculture, and home economics. From time to time there is discussion about making certain of these professional programs of education entirely graduate professional education, but my guess is that undergraduate professional education is with us for a long time to come.

In contrast with these undergraduate professional programs of education, there then began to appear in this country both graduate professional education and graduate education. In general, there are three or four professional education programs that are now firmly fixed as being graduate in character, that is, as requiring usually a baccalaureate as preprofessional educational preparation. The graduate professional fields of education now include: law, medicine, theology, and dentistry. In addition, of course, graduate education in one of the scholarly disciplines requires an undergraduate preparation.

---

1. New York: Columbia University Press, 320 pp.

58

The so-called colleges of liberal arts and the colleges of arts and sciences in a university have been left with a threefold mission: to prepare students for graduate professional education in law, medicine, and theology; to prepare students for graduate education in a discipline; and to provide a general education for those persons who desire only a baccalaureate as a kind of educational personal adornment. There are several difficulties with this situation. Apart from women students whose vocation becomes the family and whose avocation becomes community "good-works," very few students are interested in personal adornment as an educational objective. Higher education has been and is largely professional in its purposes. Accordingly, the liberal arts college and the college of arts and sciences have tended to become primarily preprofessional in their educational endeavor.

Moreover, there is no such thing as a common core of preprofessional education for the liberal arts college or the college of arts and sciences to provide. No matter how much they may avow allegiance to some concept of a general education, the medical schools look primarily for college graduates with some depth and record of achievement in the biological and physical sciences; the law schools look primarily for college graduates with some depth and record of achievement in the social sciences; and the theology schools look primarily for college graduates with some depth and record of achievement in the humanities. Furthermore, the graduate schools and colleges tend to admit students by disciplines, and each discipline is looking primarily for college graduates with a background of aptitude and accomplishment in its specialized field of study. The department of physics in a graduate school wants an undergraduate major in physics. The department of English in a graduate school wants an undergraduate major in English, and might take with appropriate dispensation an undergraduate major in history.

The separate liberal arts college, of which there are some 800 in this country, has experienced a still further pressure. I have referred to women students with a vocational objective in a family and an avocational objective in community service. Even the separate liberal arts college for women has been reluctant to accept any such formulation of purpose. In consequence, the liberal arts college finds it necessary to compromise its efforts by providing the rudiments of undergraduate professional education in teacher education, home economics, art, music, and even secretarial studies. I use the word "compromise" intentionally, because a liberal education is ordinarily thought of in

59

terms of disciplines of study rather than in terms of applied fields of professional study. Because the separate liberal arts college is usually relatively small in enrollment size and because the separate college ordinarily does not offer instruction beyond the undergraduate level, the college adds professional departments rather than professional schools to its organizational structure.

I wish to make two or three personal opinions or conclusions entirely clear. I believe professional education at the undergraduate level of instruction is entirely proper and indeed necessary. I have no intention to suggest that there is anything undesirable or inferior in undergraduate professional education. Nor do I have any illusions about the "professional" nature of such instruction provided in liberal arts colleges and in colleges of arts and sciences under the guise of being liberal or general in nature.

My contention here is only that undergraduate institutions of higher education should clarify their objectives as between general and professional education and should then relate their admissions policies and procedures to these objectives. I am well aware of difficulties that discourage or complicate any such clarification of objectives. In some instances liberal arts colleges are seeking additional enrollment and are fearful of any action that might endanger this expansion. In other instances liberal arts colleges are reluctant to diminish or limit the specialized education they offer.

I think it is fair to say that the most selective liberal arts colleges and the most selective colleges of arts and sciences within universities are primarily engaged today in the undergraduate preparation of students for graduate professional study or graduate study. The deans of such colleges annually announce the statistics about the proportion of their graduates who have been admitted to professional or graduate study. There is even a national competition among such colleges to obtain recognition of these efforts by the award of Woodrow Wilson Foundation, National Science Foundation, or other fellowships.

The less selective liberal arts colleges must afford their students the opportunity to claim some professional preparation at the undergraduate level in order to improve their employability upon completion of their baccalaureate program. This can usually be done by providing some minimum number of courses in education, business, or fine arts.

In this whole process either preprofessional or professional education has had its triumph in the undergraduate curriculum. The idea of a general undergraduate education that would seek to acquaint students

60

with the breadth of man's intellectual interests and accomplishments has largely been neglected or abandoned. There are only a few scholars who lament the loss and even fewer who believe that the loss can be recovered.

Much as I personally wish that the idea of a general education might find some favor and some active pursuit in liberal arts colleges and colleges of arts and sciences, my primary concern is to plead for a clarification, indeed, an integrity, of undergraduate educational objective. Why not acknowledge, if indeed this is its purpose, that a college is seeking to prepare its students for admission to professional and graduate study? Admission could and should then be appropriately articulated with this purpose. Why not acknowledge in certain instances that the objective of a college is to prepare its students for certain professional fields of employment, with a particular curriculum and a particular kind of student consistent with this objective? And then there just might still be here and there, as indeed there are to my knowledge, a few liberal arts colleges still devoted to the goal of a general education.

The third set of choices—after a college decides whether it is to be residential or urban and whether it will provide general or professional undergraduate education—has to do with the attitude of the institution toward the personal life of undergraduate students. Essentially there are two possibilities for a college or university to assume in its relationship with students. One possibility is to announce and enforce close supervision of a student's social activity. The other possibility is to assert that a student's social activity is beyond the scope of institutional concern. There are various gradations between these two positions, to be sure, and the present is a time when a good many different compromises are being made.

The problem of supervision of undergraduate students arose primarily as a result of the residential nature of the eighteenth- and nineteenth-century colleges. Supervision of students has always been a relatively unimportant concern for the urban college or university in this century. When the students were collected on campuses during the first half of the nineteenth century, and were usually housed in buildings built and owned by the college, various regulations about student conduct were provided. I have read such regulations for one college as they were promulgated in the 1830s. The restrictions are wonderful to behold.

In the 1830s student conduct regulations were written in consider-

61

able detail and covered a wide variety of behavior. In those days students meant mostly men, since the joys of coeducation were still ahead for most colleges. Students were expected to rise at 6 a.m. and attend morning prayers. They were to conduct themselves as gentlemen, dress conservatively, avoid boisterous language and conduct, refrain from quarreling with townspeople. Students were expected to keep their rooms clean and not to cook meals on their coal stoves. Students were forbidden to wear dirks or to engage in duels. Students were not to keep spiritous liquors in their rooms or to frequent taverns. Students were not to attend dances. There was no mention of not entertaining women in student rooms—the very act was preposterous to consider—but there was an admonition to avoid any relationship with lewd women.

From such beginnings student conduct regulations have evolved over the years, complicated by the presence and then the inundation of women students. At various times there were student revolts against and student arguments about the restrictive nature of college or university rules. I recall my father-in-law, who graduated from college in 1904, telling me with some glee how as a college student he had belonged to a secret dancing club! At the beginning of this century, as at its end, many student conduct rules existed to be evaded by enterprising students.

Today there is a whole new subdivision of psychology that is concerned with the behavior of undergraduate students and a whole new professional field of study for careers in student counseling. The present generation of students is attacking college and university regulations, which smack of parental authority, and the permissive attitude of many family relationships has undermined many collegiate standards for student conduct. Restrictions on the use of automobiles, on the use of alcoholic beverages, on women students visiting men students in their rooms, on closing hours of women's residence halls, on off-campus political or other activity, on campus social activities and meetings—all of these are the stuff of extensive student argument on every residential campus in America.

There is one aspect of this whole subject that I believe deserves more careful attention than it has thus far received. This is the impact of the presence or absence of student supervision on student academic performance. It is my personal observation that a permissive social environment on a residential campus results in the academic failure of many freshman and sophomore students. I admit that this observation

62

is limited and not systematic. I do believe that this is a matter on which colleges need more careful and controlled observation, experimentation, findings, and conclusions than they have at the present time.

Moreover, colleges seem to know very little about the actual family circumstances of a good or adequate cross section of American students. The in-depth studies of Nevitt Sanford and his associates at Vassar during the 1950s are interesting but scarcely provide conclusions based on a representative sample of college students. It is possible that more students than some may believe who enter residential campuses do so from homes where there has been a good deal of parental supervision, supervision that is provided more by exhortation and expectation than by rigorous restrictions. It is true that some students are more concerned in college with punishing a parent or demonstrating their emancipation from parental control than with demonstrating intellectual capacity.

Personally, I have a good deal of sympathy with the point of view that says that a college is concerned primarily with the intellectual development of students and not with their emotional maturity. The difficulty is that emotions do affect academic performance, and the individual student as a person must build an integrated behavior pattern that combines cognitive performance with social performance.

I fear that few colleges or universities have found a very satisfactory solution to this problem of supervised education for the undergraduate student. Student conduct regulations are the product of historical modification, hastened by current student demands. Too often these regulations reflect an institutional reaction to various pressures rather than a rational product of educational expectations.

I am particularly concerned about the consequence of this situation on the admissions process for the colleges and universities. They have concentrated attention on academic ability or promise and have become fairly proficient in judging the intellectual potential of prospective students. They have not made similar progress in their capacity to gauge the social or emotional potential of students to handle their academic objectives within the institutional pattern of expected student behavior. Indeed, I am inclined to say that they have given very little attention to this subject.

There has been some discussion in recent years about personality testing or personality screening. The very words arouse certain fears. It is said that personality testing is an invasion of privacy, or that personality testing will establish behavioral norms that will discriminate

63

against individuality and creativity. There is a fear that personality or psychological screening will carry with it an implication of abnormal condition for the rejected. Such an implication might be more devastating to students and parents than nonadmission based on insufficient academic promise. One can continue the list of objections almost indefinitely.

A few years ago as a university administrator I became concerned about the problem of how to determine whether students admitted to our campus would readily adjust to the living conditions of our residence halls. Our staff had extensive discussions of the subject in which our university psychiatrist participated. In the end we agreed that there were no certain or even partially certain methods by which to evaluate student capacity to integrate the academic program and the behavioral standards of the university.

Nonetheless, I remain convinced that colleges and universities can and should do more to define the behavioral standards they expect and define these with some care and reasonable relation to reality. In addition, colleges and universities should make these behavioral standards a part of their admissions process. With some practice and effort, they might do better than they do at present on this score. But the obstacles are great, and I have no desire to underestimate them.

There are two concluding observations that I would like to set forth. One has to do with the student role in the admissions process. The other has to do with admission as a contractual agreement between institution and student.

Colleges often overlook the fact that the admissions process begins with an act of choice or self-selection on the part of the high school graduate or his family. The high school senior—usually nine months before graduation—must decide on one or more colleges or universities where he wishes to seek admission. To be sure, some colleges and universities utilize alumni or even staff in the recruitment of high school seniors of special talent, whether this talent be academic, dramatic, musical, or athletic. For the vast majority of good and average young persons, the prospective student must first seek the college. The college or university then makes its choices from among its applicants.

For a long time, administrators, admissions officers, and others have been saying that there is too little knowledge or realistic appraisal evident in this act of choice by high school seniors. The ambitions or loyalties of parents, the friendly interest of high school teachers, the advice of counselors, the choice of close friends—all of these factors

64

are of major influence in determining the colleges or universities to which high school seniors apply. To some extent, of course, seniors do make their own selection based on the reputation of individual institutions and on their own interests.

If colleges, whether separate or parts of universities, were to define their academic and social objectives with some care, they could hope that prospective students would be better able to make their initial selections. The publication of the academic profiles of previously admitted and enrolled students is not sufficient in itself. Colleges need to state forthrightly what kind of students they want, if they are selecting some applicants and rejecting others. Moreover, it would be helpful if these statements were formulated with some exactness for a wide range of academic and personality factors related to the educational objectives of the particular college.

Finally, there is one other aspect of the admissions process that I strongly believe deserves more attention. The act of admission is a kind of contract between student and institution. The institution agrees to accept the individual and to provide him or her with a certain kind of educational opportunity. I believe the student properly has a legitimate source of complaint and of bitterness if the institution does not fulfill its commitment in this contractual arrangement. On the other hand, by accepting the offer of admission, the student also enters into a contractual agreement with the institution. He or she agrees to meet the academic standards established by the institution in order to obtain a degree and to accept the behavioral standards established by the institution governing social activity on the institution's property.

I am not suggesting that students can be required to contract away their basic rights of freedom of speech or of orderly presentation of grievances or of peaceful assembly. I am suggesting that a college or university may reasonably expect students to meet their obligations under a contract with the institution or ask students to withdraw if they break the contract.

But if the admissions process is to become in fact a contract as I believe it is indeed in essence, then I think the contract must be far more specific than it now is, and the colleges and universities must do more than they have done thus far to define their educational objectives and the standards of behavior they find related to those objectives. The time for such better definition is now.

Recognizing the Expanding Role of
Junior Colleges in Higher Education

Edmund J. Gleazer Jr.

This month of June 1967, a resolution was adopted by the legislature of the State of Florida and signed by the governor of that state that recognized that with the establishment of the final junior college area in Florida the Master Plan envisioned by the Community College Council in 1957 had been completed. When the new institution opens in the fall of 1969 the state will have put community college services within commuting distance of 99.6 percent of the population. In September of this year 26 of the 28 institutions will be in operation and will serve more than 91 percent of the state's population. By this action Florida becomes the first to make junior college services accessible to almost everyone who lives in the state. That this development took place in a systematic and orderly fashion is as noteworthy as the fact that it was done in a decade.

I refer to Florida's achievement not only because it deserves recognition but because the pattern of junior college services found there will be replicated in most of the states within the next few years. And this fact is of consequence to those responsible for planning college admissions policies in the decade ahead.

Although junior colleges have been a part of the American educational scene since the beginning of this century, their importance in terms of numbers of students served has developed only recently. (In *Planning College Policy for the Critical Decade Ahead*, published by the College Entrance Examination Board in 1958,[1] there was scarcely any reference to junior colleges.) I want to refer specifically to four states, California, Florida, New York, and Illinois, but must say again, this is a national development. Very few states do not have either junior colleges or plans for them. I can give some illustrations of what is happening. Three years ago Harrisburg Area Community College was opened. It was the first such college in Pennsylvania; this fall there will be 12. They will enroll 18,000 students, and the growth curve is zooming upward. A network of 22 junior colleges is planned for Virginia. New Jersey will have county colleges in most parts of the state. By 1975 there will be as many as 1,000 public junior colleges and 300 in-

---

1. New York: 116 pp.

dependent and church-related junior colleges in this country. Enrollment by that year may exceed three million. In several of the most highly populated states well over half of the students beginning college work will do so in junior colleges. There are 1.5 million students in some 850 junior colleges this year. More than 50 junior colleges opened last September. More than 50 will open this September. And more than 200 are in process of establishment. Most will open within the next three years.

These developments are in line with recommendations made by many national commissions to the effect that a nationwide system of free public education through two years beyond high school be established.

There seems little question about the remarkable growth of junior colleges. What does this mean for college admissions? What kinds of information are required for planning? Some of these questions occur:

1. What are enrollment trends in the junior colleges of representative states? What proportion of the students are entering junior colleges as compared with other institutions? What projections exist? Do states have policies and programs regarding distribution of college students now and during the decade ahead to various kinds of colleges and universities? Is there any noticeable proportionate cutback on the number of lower-division students served by the four-year institutions? As a matter of policy, will this develop during the next 10 years?

2. Who goes to junior colleges? What is known about the academic characteristics of these students?

3. How many students are transferring from junior colleges to four-year institutions?

4. In general, what are current admissions policies in junior colleges? What trends are discernible?

5. What policies and procedures have developed in respect to articulation between the junior colleges and four-year institutions?

Enrollment Trends in Relation to Other Institutions

In Florida, 33 percent of all first-time, in-college, on-campus students enrolled in the state university system in 1957. The same year, 46.5 percent enrolled in private institutions and 20.5 percent in Florida's public junior colleges. As Figure 1 shows, in 1966 about 15 percent were in the state university system and 22.2 percent in the private institutions, and the percentage of enrollees in the public junior colleges had increased to 62.8 percent.

With respect to total enrollments, Florida expects the public junior

Figure 1. *Florida Public Junior Colleges:*
Distribution of All First-Time, In-College, On-Campus Students
among Florida Institutions of Higher Learning,
Fall 1957—Fall 1966

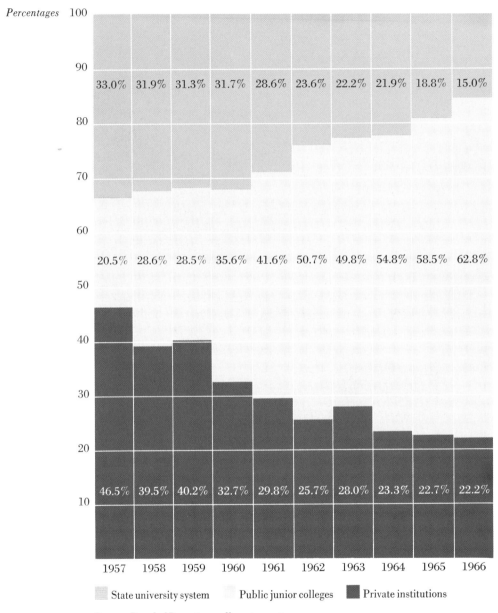

State university system   Public junior colleges   Private institutions

Source: Board of Regents enrollment reports

68

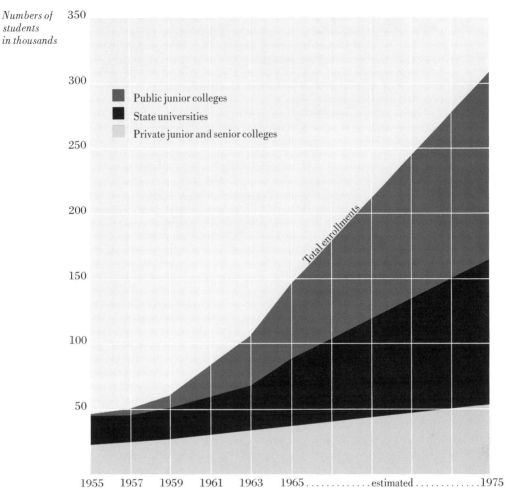

Figure 2. State of Florida: Fall Enrollments in Higher Education
1955-1975 (Est.)

Numbers of
students
in thousands

Public junior colleges
State universities
Private junior and senior colleges

Total enrollments

1955   1957   1959   1961   1963   1965..............estimated.............1975

colleges to have 47 percent of the state's enrollment in 1975, the state universities 36 percent, and the private junior and senior colleges 17 percent. As Figure 2 shows, this compares with 40 percent, 35 percent, and 25 percent respectively in 1965.

In New York the community college has been described as the basic plank in the state's program of higher education. Although not on the dramatic scale found in Florida, the proportion of students enrolled in New York two-year colleges both public and private is projected to increase from 17.2 percent of full-time enrollment in 1966-67 to 26.8 percent by 1975 and up to 30 percent in 1980. According to studies by the State Education Department[2] the role of the private institutions will likely stabilize at a much higher level in New York than in other states. Incidentally, just to show the size of the total job to be done, full-time enrollment in 1980-81 is projected to be approximately three times as large as in 1960-61 in all institutions. Enrollment in four-year colleges will be comprised of a larger proportion of upper-class students than in the past as the community colleges serve a larger portion of the students in the first two years and transfer becomes more common for students seeking the baccalaureate degree. State University of New York estimates that in 1970 upper-division students will constitute 57 percent of undergraduate enrollment in university centers and 50 percent in university colleges.

California restricts admission to the university to those high school graduates who are in the top 12 percent; and the California state colleges admit those in the top 33.33 percent. All the public four-year colleges are working toward a 40 percent lower-division, 60 percent upper-division ratio. The Master Plan for Higher Education suggested that by 1975 the distribution of lower-division enrollment should be 75 percent in junior colleges, 17.5 percent in state colleges, and 7.5 percent at the University of California.[3] Seventy-five percent of all full-time lower-division students attending a public college in California are enrolled in a junior college. The rate of growth[4] for the past five years has

2. E. L. Eckles, *Actual and Projected Enrollment in New York State Institutions of Higher Education.* Albany: Office of Planning in Higher Education, State Education Department, 1966, 21 pp.

3. Arthur M. Jensen, in a letter to the author. Sacramento: Department of Education —State of California, May 11, 1967.

4. Coordinating Council for Higher Education, *The Flow of Students Into, Among, and Through the Public Institutions of Higher Education in California.* Sacramento: Bureau of Junior College Education, February 1966, 61 pp.

been 9 percent per year. Estimates call for future growth in enrollments for the next 10 years of the order of 10 percent per year. The fall 1966 enrollments in the public junior colleges of California are shown in Table 1 below.

Distribution of full-time, fall-term, lower-division enrollment among the three segments of public higher education in California for the years 1960 through 1965 and Master Plan modified projections are shown

Table 1. Fall 1966 Enrollments in California Public Junior Colleges

	Full-time	Part-time
Freshmen	145,405	70,395
Sophomores	50,585	17,819
Others, excluding adults	5,558	10,131
Total	201,548	98,345
Total graded enrollment		299,893
Total adults		271,014
Grand total		570,907

Table 2. California: Distribution of Full-time, Fall-term, Lower-division Enrollment among the Three Segments of Public Higher Education, 1960-65*

Segment	Actual						Master Plan modified projections	
	1960	1961	1962	1963	1964	1965	1965	1975
University	11.5%	11.1%	11.1%	11.4%	10.3%	10.1%† (11.1)‡	8.6%	7.5%
State colleges	19.2	19.9	19.9	20.2	19.4	16.1† (15.9)‡	19.5	17.5
Junior colleges	69.3	69.0	69.0	68.4	70.3	73.8† (73.0)‡	71.9	75.0

* Coordinating Council for Higher Education, *The Flow of Students Into, Among, and Through the Public Institutions of Higher Education in California.* Sacramento: Bureau of Junior College Education, February 1966, 61 pp.

† Based on a 56-unit dividing line between lower and upper division for the university's 1965 enrollment.

‡ Based on a 60-unit dividing line between lower and upper division for the university's 1965 enrollment.

71

in Table 2. Very recently the Coordinating Council was requested by the state legislature to study to what extent the senior institutions should drop their lower-level programs.

The Master Plan for Higher Education in Illinois[5] adopted by the General Assembly in 1965 projects an increase in junior college enrollment from about 67,000 students in 1966-67 to 274,000 by 1980. A statewide system of public junior colleges is being developed with amazing speed. Enrollment policies of the plan state that by "1970-71 the lower-division enrollments of the presently established public senior institutions [will] be stabilized so that thereafter no permanent additional enrollments (beyond the full-time-equivalent number enrolled in the Fall term of 1970) be permitted in the lower-divisions of these institutions, . . ."

Who Goes to Junior Colleges?

Junior college spokesmen have maintained that the public community college taps new pools of talent—that a large proportion of their student population would not be in college if it were not for the accessibility of the institutions, the broad variety of programs offered, and the "open-door" admissions policies. Studies in several states come up with much the same kind of information about junior college students. They represent all levels of ability ranging from the very low to the very high. Florida reports that the graduating classes usually have many examples of fathers and sons, mothers and daughters, and even occasionally grandmothers and granddaughters graduating at the same time. About 70 percent of the students in that state come from families that have no previous college experience. They appear to be less certain about their educational goals than a similar group attending the university. In the fall of 1967 a major study will be initiated in Florida of all students beginning junior colleges and the universities that should result in more specific information about student characteristics than is now available.

In California the junior college students represent a cross section of the population in most communities, although students from homes of professionals and executives are underrepresented. A typical freshman enters junior college with, generally, lower academic ability than an entering freshman at a four-year college. Based on a sample of all enter-

---

5. State of Illinois Board of Higher Education, *A Master Plan—Phase II: For Higher Education in Illinois.* Springfield: Board of Higher Education, December 1966, 68 pp.

72

ing first-time freshmen enrolled in California junior colleges in the fall term of 1965, 27.17 percent were eligible for state colleges, and 7.94 percent were eligible for the University of California. The students ranged from 16 to 85 years. Their median age was 21. Most lived at home. More than 10 percent of the students lacked high school diplomas.

Medsker[6] reports that nationally fewer than half of the students in junior colleges are enrolled on a full-time basis although nearly three-fourths of the students in the private institutions are carrying 12 or more units per semester. Two-thirds of the full-time students in public junior colleges and 61 percent of those in the private institutions are freshmen.

Illinois[7] statistics confirm other reports with respect to the high proportion of part-time students in junior colleges. A report in 1967 shows 67,526 students distributed as follows: full-time freshmen 20.3 percent, full-time sophomores 13.7 percent, full-time unclassified students 1.3 percent, part-time freshmen 33.3 percent, part-time sophomores 11.5 percent, and part-time unclassified students 10.8 percent. Fewer than one-half, or 44.3 percent, of all students enrolled in public junior colleges in Illinois are full-time students. Only 25.3 percent of the students are sophomores; 62.6 percent are freshmen. There are other data from Illinois that indicate that large numbers of students are leaving the public junior college prior to the completion of a program that would entitle them to a degree or a certificate.

This observation is supported by other very recent reports brought to my attention by Dale Tillery at the Center for Research and Development in Higher Education at the University of California. His findings have profound implications for university plans that take into account both the size and the kind of transfer population in the junior colleges.

At this point there is trouble with words—words like "persistence," "attrition," and "dropout." These imply that institutional objectives and student objectives are met as the student *completes* a two- or four-

---

6. National Committee for Appraisal and Development of Junior College Student Personnel Programs, *Junior College Student Personnel Programs—Appraisal and Development* (A Report to Carnegie Corporation of New York). Washington, D.C.: American Association of Junior Colleges, November 1965, approx. 200 pp.

7. Ernest F. Anderson and James S. Spencer, *Report of Selected Data and Characteristics—Illinois Public Junior Colleges, 1966-67.* Springfield: Illinois Junior College Board, 1967, 107 pp.

year program. As indicated below, some questions must be raised about this assumption.

Dr. Tillery reports that persistence records of 22,322 students from 57 junior colleges in 21 states who entered in the fall of 1961 were kept through the spring semester of 1965. Approximately 66 percent of these students were either dismissed or withdrew before completing 60 units of credit during this period. Actually, slightly more than 54 percent were dismissed. One-third of the students either completed the associate degree (25 percent) or withdrew with 60 units or more of credit. Approximately 50 percent of the students withdrew before beginning the fourth quarter at their junior colleges. More than 20 percent of these junior college students withdrew before or at the close of the first semester.

Dr. Tillery cautions that considerable variability in attrition rates exists among junior colleges. The urban institutions with their heavy component of students from educationally and economically deficient homes have special problems in holding power.

When compared with data from major attrition studies in four-year institutions, which over the years would tend to indicate that approximately 50 percent of the students who begin in senior institutions do not complete their four-year programs, the junior-college attrition rate looks shocking. However, Dr. Tillery and others ask, "When is a 'dropout' not a dropout?"

"First, when the student is a 'push-out.' Many junior colleges continue to invite students into the open door whom they are not prepared to educate and for whom they do not have either proper programs or guidance. These students leave in large numbers very early after entering the institutions and should be seen as 'push-outs' rather than dropouts. Secondly, there would seem to be a rather large number of students in junior colleges who have achieved some goals, however personal, which make them employable or which add up to a satisfying experience, even for their brief stay at the junior college. In some cases the short-run certificate programs contribute to this situation. Thirdly, I suspect that there are a number of young men and women who, as a result of their brief junior college experiences, in the classroom and guidance, leave school as a step in finding themselves. We have some indication that a rather large number of these students will return to the junior college or other education at a later date. A last group which must be considered in interpreting the heavy junior college loss are those students for whom formal redirection efforts through guidance

74

and course exploration have been successful. This frequently results in shifting from an inappropriate educational and vocational goal to more immediate employment or deferment of education."[8]

More and better information about why some students drop out of higher education entirely or migrate among institutions will come out of the SCOPE project that Dr. Tillery is now directing. SCOPE (School to College: Opportunities for Postsecondary Education) is a follow-up study of some 35,000 high school seniors as they move into work and college.

Regardless of the reasons for the high attrition rates in junior colleges—and there is a great deal more to be known about this phenomenon—from the standpoint of university admissions policies it is clear that if a million students begin their work in junior colleges in 1968 the universities do not need to base their planning on accepting almost one million students transferring from junior colleges in 1970. There is, however, reason to judge that a larger proportion of these students will transfer as the junior college broadens its programs, improves its counseling, and strengthens its instructional process to do a more effective job with the very broad spectrum of students' aptitudes, interests, and achievements.

According to Medsker,[9] Project Talent offers the most conclusive evidence concerning the academic ability of a nationwide sample of junior college students. The conclusion drawn by the investigators is that the junior college freshmen are very much like high school seniors with respect to the distribution of their academic aptitude. Their mean score is very similar to that of high school seniors and is considerably below the mean for students who entered four-year institutions. However, the junior colleges appear to draw somewhat heavily from the middle range of ability and somewhat less from the upper and lower extremes. There is considerable evidence that the junior-college *transfer students* have a higher level of ability than the average high school graduate.

Except in New York State, high school graduates were found to have chosen the junior college over other types of institutions for reasons of low cost, closeness to home, and opportunity for employment while at-

---

8. Dale Tillery, in a letter to the author. Berkeley: Center for Research and Development in Higher Education, University of California, June 12, 1967.
9. National Committee for Appraisal and Development of Junior College Student Personnel, *op. cit.*

tending. In New York nearly two-thirds of the students chose the junior college because of the specialized programs offered and only one-fourth of them cited factors of cost and convenience as reasons for attending a junior college.

How Many Will Transfer to Four-Year Colleges?

The educational role of junior colleges is much broader than that of preparing students for the upper division of four-year institutions. Many of its students will be of "high risk" academically. A broad spectrum of educational options will confront a great variety of students. Through effective counseling there will be a matching of students and goals. Large numbers will achieve educational and occupational and personal objectives before completing the associate degree. Many of these will return to the community college for continuing work as needs indicate. Although increasing numbers of college and university students will have taken their first year or two in a junior college, the percentage of students not transferring is at present considerably greater than that of students who do continue a four-year program. In California about 20 percent of the entering junior college students eventually transfer to a four-year program, and about 80 percent of these are granted a four-year degree. Florida's experience has been that approximately 30 out of every 100 entering freshmen transfer to four-year colleges. This proportion has been relatively constant during the last several years. However, characteristically junior college enrollees state their intention to transfer. Nationally, two-thirds of the entering students say they will transfer. Actually, only one-third transfer within a four-year period. This means that increasing enrollment in junior colleges does not mean proportionate increase in junior-college transfer students bound for the four-year colleges. The numbers of junior college students who transfer will likely be large but not nearly as large as the enrollment increases in the junior colleges.

Admissions Policies in Junior Colleges and Apparent Trends

Publicly supported community colleges will be predominantly "open-door" institutions. However, admission to programs *within* the college will be on a selective basis. In California, all high school graduates may enter the junior colleges. In addition, the colleges may admit—and are encouraged to do so—all persons over 18 years of age who can profit from their instructional programs. Admissions policies are often defined in the enabling act that authorizes the institutions. For example,

76

in Illinois a section of the Public Junior College Act of 1965 has this specification:

"The Class I junior college districts shall admit all students qualified to complete any one of their programs including general education, transfer, occupational, technical, and terminal, as long as space for effective instruction is available. After entry, the college shall counsel and distribute the students among its programs according to their interests and abilities. Students allowed entry in college transfer programs must have ability and competence similar to that possessed by students admitted to state universities for similar programs. Entry level competence to such college transfer programs may be achieved through successful completion of other preparatory courses offered by the college."[10]

In New York State the admissions policies are broadening toward the open-door philosophy implied in the master-plan goals of the State University of New York. "These institutions (comprehensive community colleges) should be open to all high school graduates or persons with equivalent educational background, operated at low cost to the students, and located within reasonable daily commuting distance of the students' place of residence."[11]

Factors that may inhibit the "open-door policy" implementation include attitudes of junior college faculty. As one of my correspondents put it, "We find the published admission policies in harmony with the statute. I must admit that we have some faculty members who still desire that public junior colleges serve only the liberal arts and operate with a limited admission policy. Theirs is in no way a dominant voice but it does exist."

Another factor is the problem of selection when facilities and programs are not ample for all comers.

Community college leaders are predicting that during the next 10 years, the community junior colleges will offer opportunity to all persons, without regard to their previous educational experience or accomplishments, who can demonstrate that they will benefit from the educational experience available in that institution. In some state legislatures concern has been expressed for students who have experienced

10. Ernest F. Anderson and James S. Spencer, *op. cit.*
11. New York State Board of Regents, *The Comprehensive Community College: A Policy Statement of the New York State Board of Regents.* Albany: February 27, 1964, 4 pp.

difficulty previously. This concern is pointed toward the community junior college's offering these students a chance to catch up.

Articulation between Junior Colleges and Four-Year Institutions

According to T. R. McConnell, former chairman of the Center for the Study of Higher Education at the University of California, "If education beyond the fourteenth year is to be assured to students whose aptitude and achievement qualify them for it, community colleges, in addition to their several other functions, will have to prepare students for successful work in the upper divisions of four-year institutions."[12]

McConnell describes a study of transfer students by the Center:

". . . the national transfer study involved some 10,000 students, 345 two-year institutions which they entered as freshmen, and a diverse group of forty-three senior colleges and universities to which they transferred. The prediction of success of the transfer student turned out to be a complicated problem. His academic performance in the four-year college or university was the outcome of a subtle accommodation between his attributes and the characteristics of the institution he entered or the particular part of the institution in which he concentrated his studies. The success of the transfer student was a function of his characteristics, the range of alternatives open to him when he chose a senior institution, the academic standards and the total climate of the senior college to which he transferred, and the interaction between the characteristics of the student and the institution."[13]

In the study referred to, Dorothy M. Knoell and Leland L. Medsker make recommendations that have a direct bearing on university admissions policy during this next decade. They assert that the four-year colleges have an obligation to plan for the orderly accommodation of the increasing numbers of transfer students and that this obligation should be made explicit in state master plans that call for strengthened junior colleges. This means not only additional spaces at the upper-division level but also new types of programs to match the needs of the variety of junior college transferees. For example, different kinds of programs might be in order to build on junior-college occupational curriculums as technology expands. If all four-year colleges attempt to emulate the

---

12. Dorothy M. Knoell and Leland L. Medsker, *From Junior to Senior College: A National Study of the Transfer Student.* Washington, D.C.: American Council on Education, 1965, p. v.
13. *Ibid.*, p. vi.

78

major state universities in curriculum development and standards, responsibilities to the junior colleges will be neglected. The authors urge that "coordinating agencies . . . undertake the development of undergraduate curriculum master plans at an early date to insure that new opportunities will be available as needed."

Other suggestions made by Knoell and Medsker[14] that have implications for planners of admissions policies include these:

"Cease referring to programs as 'terminal' and 'transfer' and, instead, . . . recognize the student's right to be either terminal or transfer in either type of program, depending upon his achievement, abilities, and changing interests. . . .

"The proper matching of transfer student and institution at the upper division level is just as important a goal as the matching of high school graduate and institution at the freshman level. . . . More information should be obtained on a continuing basis concerning the relative success of transfer students in different types of four-year colleges and programs. More effective ways of using such information need to be conceived in counseling and admissions programs. . . .

"Both the master planners and the universities need to consider the right of the junior college graduate to transfer to *any* public four-year college. If opportunity to transfer to the major state universities is limited to those with a reasonable probability of success, the next question to be faced is the extent to which specialized majors should be developed in other types of institutions to which transfer students can be diverted. . . .

"To accommodate the heterogeneity of talent and interests which is present in the very large groups of junior college students who plan to transfer to four-year institutions, diversity of opportunity needs to be developed at the junior and senior levels. . . .

"Weak students with both subject-matter and scholarship deficiencies should probably remain in junior college for more than two years before transfer in order to catch up with their classmates who began junior college without such deficiencies. . . . For such students a three-plus-two program would probably bring greater success than a two-plus-three program, from which many students are now being dropped one year after transfer because of poor grades. . . .

"When transfer students to particular institutions have less academic ability than native students, they should not be expected to earn

---

14. *Ibid.*, pp. 89-101.

grades on a par with those of the natives. The more important question to be answered is whether transfer students with lesser ability earn grades which enable them to persist and to meet graduation requirements. If the yardstick used to measure transfer student success is the grade point average earned by native students, without controlling for differences in academic aptitude, one may expect to find that junior college students will be required to meet ever increasing admission standards for transfer. Coordinating agencies should strive to maintain a good academic 'mix' in the junior colleges, i.e., to avoid siphoning off all the best students for the four-year institutions. . . .

"In the light of the needs of the students who begin their degree programs in junior colleges, a critical examination should be made both of the current philosophy of financial aid and of the nature of existing programs. . . .

"Most students should be urged to remain in junior college until they can transfer with full upper-division standing. . . .

"A sizeable reduction in attrition could be produced by means of a better matching of transfer students and four-year colleges, with the objective of getting each student into an institution where he has a better-than-even chance of success. . . .

"Two- and four-year colleges are rapidly becoming interdependent with respect to the planned mobility of their undergraduate students. If a certain degree of autonomy in curricular matters is to be preserved, considerable attention must be given to the development of common policies and guidelines for transfer to which the various colleges in each state will subscribe."

The authors of this significant report conclude by asserting that "articulation is both a process and an attitude" and that attitude is the more important of the two, for without it there can be no workable process.

Based on the research results of the transfer study and developed through 10 state conferences involving both junior and senior college personnel, a guidelines statement toward articulation was prepared by a joint committee of the Association of American Colleges, the American Association of Junior Colleges, and the American Association of Collegiate Registrars and Admissions Officers.[15] It was incorporated in

---

15. Joint Committee on Junior and Senior Colleges, *Guidelines for Improving Articulation between Junior and Senior Colleges*. Washington, D.C.: American Council on Education, 17 pp.

80

several state plans, including those of Florida, New York, Illinois, and Virginia. Action taken by the State Council of Higher Education for Virginia in approving guidelines designed to promote the smooth transfer of students from the two-year institutions to the state's four-year colleges and universities is illustrative of that in other states.

Guidelines for Promoting Articulation Between the State-Controlled Community Colleges and Four-Year Colleges and Universities [16]

"In accord with its responsibility for the development of a coordinated system of higher education in Virginia the State Council of Higher Education at its April 3, 1967 meeting approved the following guidelines designed to promote the smooth transfer of students completing appropriate college-transfer programs in the state two-year comprehensive community colleges into the state four-year colleges and universities. The guidelines are viewed as principles and working agreements whereby the community colleges, the four-year institutions, and students will jointly and cooperatively plan baccalaureate degree opportunities. These ten statements were recommended to the Council by its Two-Year/Four-Year Articulation Advisory Committee, a 17-member group of faculty and administrative personnel representing the state-controlled four-year colleges and universities, and the state-system of comprehensive community colleges. They also received the endorsement of the State Council's General Professional Advisory Committee, a group composed of the Presidents of all the four-year state institutions of higher education and the Director of the State Department of Community Colleges.

"I. In order to assist students in evaluating their general progress and the appropriateness of their educational objectives, four-year institutions and two-year colleges should work jointly and establish systematic procedures to provide counselors and advisors with current and continuing information about comparable courses, curriculum changes, requirements for admission, student characteristics, student services, and performance of transfers.

"II. Two-year college students should be encouraged to choose as early as possible the four-year institution and program into which they expect to transfer in order to plan programs which may include all lower division requirements of the four-year institution.

"III. Performance in the college transfer program offered by two-

---

16. Richmond: State Council of Higher Education for Virginia, April 3, 1967.

year colleges is the best single predictor of success in four-year institutions and, therefore, should count heavily in the evaluation of transfer applicants.

"IV. Admissions standards of four-year institutions should be stated in such a way that two-year college students may know whether they can be considered for transfer.

"V. Transfer applicants from new two-year colleges in the process of being accredited should be evaluated on the same basis as applicants from regionally accredited two-year colleges.

"VI. The evaluation of transfer courses by four-year institutions should serve to inform the individual student who has been accepted for admission how far he has advanced toward his degree objective and what residence and subject requirements must still be met.

"VII. The satisfactory completion of an appropriate two-year associate degree transfer program should normally assure upper division standing at the time of transfer.

"VIII. Achievement and aptitude testing of transfer students may be utilized to assist in their placement at appropriate levels in various sequences of courses.

"IX. Transfer students should be given the option of satisfying graduation requirements which were in effect at four-year institutions at the time they enrolled as freshmen, subject to conditions or qualifications which apply to native students.

"X. The Two-Year/Four-Year Articulation Advisory Committee composed of representatives from public and private two-year and four-year institutions should meet at least semiannually to consider appropriate problems, suggest needed studies, and recommend to the State Council of Higher Education additional guidelines for effective articulation."

Summary Comments for Admissions Planners

1. Throughout the nation community college services will be accessible, geographically and financially.

2. Characteristics of students taking postsecondary programs will be much like those of high school graduates in general.

3. The junior or community college in admissions policies relating to the institution will be relatively nonselective although selective in respect to programs.

4. The availability of an "open-door" community college to most high school graduates may suggest that some four-year colleges and

82

universities become more selective in admission of freshman students.

5. Some four-year institutions may plan a proportionate decrease in lower-division enrollment. Some may terminate lower-division enrollments.

6. Increasing numbers of university applicants will have had one or two years of previous college experience.

7. Articulation machinery will be required to facilitate the flow of students from two- to four-year colleges.

8. A receiving institution will acknowledge through its programs, procedures, and policies that the junior-college transfer students may be different in characteristics and experience from the freshman enrollees.

9. Admissions officers may utilize as predictive factors a student's junior college experience rather than high school record.

10. The rapidly developing spectrum of two-year occupational programs will have implications for the admissions officer. How will these programs be viewed in respect to transfer credit?

11. An increasing number of students will come to the universities having taken academic work different in sequence, content, and setting from that of students who enter as freshmen. How will the university deal with this large heterogenous group?

The junior college has evolved to meet an apparent educational need —broader educational opportunities through factors of proximity, economy, and variety of programs. Within this next decade more than half of the people starting their college work will do so in these institutions. One-third of these or more will seek entry to four-year institutions. Admissions policies and procedures are required that not only recognize the role and identity and worth of both the two-year and four-year institutions but facilitate movement from one institution to another when it is time for students to make this change.

The junior college can be an educational instrument of tremendous worth to individuals and the nation. The extent to which its potential is fulfilled will be conditioned by its function as part of a total system of education. Both the junior colleges and the universities have a responsibility to see that it works as a part of that system.

83

Not the Traditional Student but
Almost Everyone Else

Jack N. Arbolino

Wise lovers know the incommunicability of love—so do wise poets, and maybe even better. It's a safe bet that for every poem that effectively treats the wonder of love by suggestion, ten thousand fail because they grab the subject by the throat and shake it up and down. I am convinced that one of the quickest ways to destroy something beautiful is to write an essay about it or examine it under a microscope. Wonderful things like love or beauty or the College-Level Examination Program are not always easy to talk about—but I'll try.

The College-Level Examination Program (CLEP) may be the College Board's most important contribution to higher education. If this seems an extravagant claim, particularly in the light of the Board's history, which some have said is not without significant achievement, I suppose I can only say it is not mine alone. The president of the Board, Richard Pearson, feels it; the trustees of the Board feel it, and so does the Council on College-Level Examinations, the Program's advisory group. The Carnegie Corporation of New York has given us generous support, the Federation of Regional Accrediting Commissions and the Commission on Accreditation of Service Experiences have given their endorsement, and we are getting a good response from the colleges.

What is this new program in which we place such great hope? It's a long overdue program based on credit by examination. The idea is almost as old as the ocean's roar. From the Redbricks of London to the University of Missouri in 1876, to Buffalo and Chicago in the thirties, the fire of the idea has flickered, but a national system has never caught on. We have had studies by the score, and always before us is the fact that our present means for assessing intellectual achievement are plainly inadequate. For more than 30 years it has been clear that the correlation between knowledge possessed and time spent in class in any given subject is unbelievably low. In 1937, the president of The Carnegie Foundation for the Advancement of Teaching called William S. Learned and Ben D. Wood's, *The Student and His Knowledge*,[1] a "landmark in the passing of the system of units and credits

---

1. New York: The Carnegie Foundation for the Advancement of Teaching, 1938, 406 pp.

which, useful as it was a third of a century ago, is not good enough for American education today." Lewis Terman said of that same work that it "set the stage for a thoroughgoing reform of collegiate education." That was many years ago, and current problems and opportunities cry for action that has not been taken. The College-Level Examination Program can help break some bonds that tied American education then and tie it now. But with all our hopes there is really nothing very radical about the Program, except that it makes sense. If one accepts the thesis that to treasure learning is to transmit it and see it used, then it's no great leap to the assumption that scholarly and societal goals are not antithetical. We aren't trying to start a national university. Credit will be given by the colleges, and the Program won't even tell them at what scores they ought to give credit. That's their business.

Seven years ago as director of the Advanced Placement Program, I gave a talk for the Association for Higher Education called "Establishing and Maintaining Better Curricular Articulation Between Secondary and Higher Education." I said then, "We must scrutinize credentials and devise tests that will yield enough information to enable us to certify, place, and divide into sections *all* students in *all* subjects from grades 11 to 14 and maybe beyond. The development of such a testing program is a frightening thought and a tremendous task, but I know of no more important job in American education. Admissions and placement must be refined where they have been rudimentary, protean where they have been procrustean."

That job, as I have just indicated, is now under way, but before describing it, I'd like to say a few words about the Advanced Placement Program and its relationship to the College-Level Examination Program. The College-Level Examination Program owes much to the Advanced Placement Program. Indeed the Advanced Placement Program, which one might say should have followed or been a by-product of an established, truly articulated placement program, preceded it, and so the Advanced Placement Program was and is the child that is father of the man. If Advanced Placement entered the world trailing clouds of celestial glory, we're coming in with a rising wind at our back.

The Advanced Placement Program, for historical and political purposes, developed into an exciting showpiece for the Board. It is an important contribution to American education that has not only rattled some assumptions but has enabled high school students and teachers to work to their highest capacity and then see that work recognized.

In 11 years the number of schools offering Advanced Placement courses has grown from 104 to 2,518 and the candidates from 1,200 to 38,000. This is substantial, but still the Advanced Placement Program reaches so few. There remains the larger world of students, schools, and colleges untouched by it. How does.the College-Level Examination Program affect that world, and what is its relationship to the Advanced Placement Program?

The Advanced Placement Program is part of the College-Level Examination Program under the umbrella of the Council on College-Level Examinations.

There are certain assumptions about the two programs.

1. The College-Level Examination Program should not diminish or hinder the Advanced Placement Program. The reverse, of course, is also true.

2. Although the concept of credit by examination obtains in both programs, the Advanced Placement Examinations are developed with a course description in mind and the bulk of the candidates have followed the course of study suggested.

3. The College-Level Examination Program presupposes no particular pattern of preparation, nor does it expect of the candidates any common background.

4. The College Board should bar no candidate regardless of age or previous academic background from Advanced Placement or College-Level Examinations. Where similar examinations exist in both programs, institutions that will receive score reports will decide on eligibility for credit.

The College-Level Examination Program has other implications for secondary schools. If a high school is regarded as a community school, a place used freely for all the needs of living and learning, it must be regarded as an agency that affects the economy, the productivity, and the social, intellectual, and even spiritual development of persons of all ages.

As the manifold needs of a community are pursued, the College-Level Examination Program can be a means to help housewives, dropouts, and professionally, technically, and career-minded adults to meet licensing requirements, to qualify for higher positions, and perhaps (and most important) to meet personal requirements of self-fulfillment.

To take only two of these groups, the housewives and the dropouts, how more readily can we speed the housewives' return or entrance to teaching? And how better can we salvage the resources the dropouts represent? Is not a program of credit by examination our most effective way to inspire, sustain, or, as is so often needed, restore continuity in education?

In recent years the Advanced Placement Program has rattled some assumptions, and admissions and placement have become, if not refined, at least less rudimentary. But they are still more procrustean than protean. If we as educators are not ready to provide access and opportunity, to install some supplementary means for recognizing and rewarding achievement, to try to do a more accurate job of placement, we may spend the rest of our lives trying to catch up with the past. I prefer to think that we shall do something to shape the future.

The College-Level Examination Program was conceived to serve not the traditional students who move from secondary school to colleges but almost everyone else interested in continuing his education and getting formal recognition for it. As if this were not enough, it can also serve colleges that deal only with traditional students.

The Program began in 1965 with the broad purpose of developing a national system of placement and credit by examination specifically directed to higher education. The students floating free outside the changing structure of higher education and the students in transition within it were our main concern. The Program has four major objectives: to provide a national program of examinations that can be used to evaluate nontraditional college-level education, specifically including independent study and correspondence work; to stimulate colleges and universities to develop appropriate procedures for the placement, accreditation, and admission of transfer students; to provide colleges and universities with a means by which to evaluate their programs and their students' achievement; to assist adults who wish to continue their education in order to meet licensing requirements or qualify for higher positions.

The first examinations offered by the College-Level Examination Program are the former Comprehensive College Tests, originally developed by Educational Testing Service and now sponsored by the College Board. Incidentally, one of the best-kept secrets in American education is that the College Board and ETS are separate organizations. We *do* work together, and the Board is grateful to ETS for the work it has done on this Program, but I want to emphasize that the College-Level Examination Program is a College Board program, and the direction and responsibility for it are ours. To return to the examinations, then, there are two types: General Examinations and Subject Examinations.

The General Examinations are:

English Composition

Humanities (subscores in Fine Arts and Literature)

Mathematics (subscores in Basic Skills and Course Content)

Natural Sciences (subscores in Biological Science and Physical Science)

Social Sciences–History (subscores in Social Sciences and History)

They are intended to provide a comprehensive measure of undergraduate achievement in the five basic areas of the liberal arts listed above. They are not intended to measure advanced training in any specific discipline, but rather to assess a student's knowledge of fundamental facts and concepts, his ability to perceive relationships, and his understanding of the basic principles of the subject. The content of the General Examinations is similar to the content of those subjects ordinarily included in the program of study required of most general education students in the first two years of college.

The Subject Examinations are:

American Government

Analysis and Interpretation of Literature

English Composition

General Chemistry

General Psychology

Geology

Introductory Calculus

Introductory Economics

Introductory Sociology

Tests and Measurements

Western Civilization

The Subject Examinations are essentially end-of-course tests developed for widely taught undergraduate courses. They measure understanding of basic facts and concepts, as well as the ability to apply such understanding to the solution of problems and the interpretation of materials. Questions that require of a student only rote recall are avoided.

All the examinations are developed by examining committees consisting of faculty members of colleges and universities. Committee members define the topics to be covered, review the test specifications, prepare and review test questions, and develop standards for grading

88

the essay questions of the Subject Examinations. The committees are assisted by test-development specialists. To set overall specifications, to formulate standards, to appraise existing examinations, and to initiate new ones, panels of distinguished teachers have been appointed in three areas: English, mathematics–science, and social sciences. Consultants, charged with the same functions, have been retained to guide examining committees in the five Subject Examinations being developed this year: Educational Psychology, History of American Education, Marketing, Money and Banking, and Statistics. It is anticipated that all these examinations will be available in 1968. Plans call for the development every year of new examinations in new fields. In the identification of these fields we need advice, and we invite suggestions. This is an earnest invitation; we are not interested in proving any particular theory of ours but in meeting practical needs.

The tests have been developed with care, but the best tests in the world are not worth much unless they are used and the results intelligently applied to helping students gain the education they want and need. The Program recognizes that unaffiliated and independent students need help. I suspect, too, that the transfer process at all levels isn't as smooth as we say it is. At conventions the talk one hears over coffee and in the corridors is not the same as the speeches from the platforms.

What is the background of the problems we face? Even casual observation reveals some complex conclusions about education. Knowledge is expanding. Today's college graduates in relation to what they know of what exists to be known may be the poorest prepared ever. Adult education will swell in the next 20 years (28 million adults are engaged in some form of education now). Education stands between a man and a good job more flat-footedly and formidably than it ever has before. Two-year colleges, opportunities for independent study, and the population of the United States are all multiplying at a tremendous rate.

Moreover, observation and research show that college preparatory work is better than it ever has been. More students are moving from two-year to four-year colleges and transferring from one four-year college to another. Industry, the armed forces, and business have developed both educational programs and training programs that match in size the entire college and university system (there are 32,000 programs other than those in colleges and universities that enroll high school graduates). Unless education truly becomes a way of life, our national economy and our social structure will be done irreparable harm. And, as if all this growth and change weren't enough, there is the old maxim that the more education a person has, the more he wants.

To cope with these overwhelming challenges, the Board is developing the College-Level Examination Program. This project, guided by a distinguished Council on which two-year colleges have strong representation, hopes to help provide more educational opportunities for more Americans. Publications, research, test development, and demonstration projects are under way. At the moment it is possible to administer tests only at institutions, but a plan to establish centrally located testing centers across the country is being developed. The Federation of Regional Accrediting Commissions has approved the principle of using the examinations to validate unconventional instruction, and the Commission on Accreditation of Service Experiences has recommended that the examinations be employed as a basis for awarding credit and advanced standing to servicemen who are returning to college.

Here are some actual examples of how the Program is currently being used.

1. One of the country's major state universities located in the Midwest uses the tests to provide alternate channels for meeting institutional requirements for graduation.

2. In the South, a private college requires all students to take the General Examinations at the end of the sophomore year. The results are used to assist transfer and continuing students in the transition to upper-class study.

3. A public junior college in the East compares its graduating sophomores with the national norms on the basis of the examination scores and also uses the test as a counseling tool for work with these graduating sophomores.

4. The General Examinations are being used by an urban college in a large eastern city to provide information for use in the admission and placement of adults in a special, beginning college program.

5. An experimentally oriented and only recently established institution in the South has found the tests of value in providing information for the educational counseling of enrolled students and for research.

6. The United States Armed Forces Institute (USAFI) administers the examinations to servicemen (40,000 last year) and reports scores to colleges, thus recognizing the examinations' value in measuring the

90

continued growth and development of individuals in the military service.

7. A liberal arts coeducational university in the East recognizes superior preparation and accomplishment of its entering freshmen by means of the General Examinations, and grants waiver of credit for certain first- and second-year requirements.

8. A major western state college insures basic levels of achievement in the liberal arts of students in secondary education programs who seek to enroll for student teaching by requiring them to score above a certain level on all five General Examinations.

9. A number of organizations and agencies other than colleges and universities use the tests to provide measures of the college equivalency needed for a technical position or promotion to a better job.

It might be well to stress the Program's possible use by junior colleges by listing various ways the examinations could help two-year college students and administrators.

1. In the counseling of graduating sophomores, both transfer and career students.

2. In institutional self-evaluation of standards or achievement levels.

3. In the transfer process of career students who decide after graduation to transfer.

4. In the assessment of adults who wish to obtain the Associate in Arts degree, as well as transfer-minded adults such as veterans and housewives.

5. In the admission of adults.

With so many uses, with such support, and with the obvious merit it possesses, how can the Program fail? Easily. It can fail out of sloth, and pride, and gross indifference, and the last is the most likely. It can fail because of the vast and bitter loneliness of the unaffiliated student, the ponderous locks of educational tradition, and the Talmudic tangles of curricular diversity. It can also fail through mismanagement, but we won't dwell on that.

The College-Level Examination Program is designed to serve current and changing modes of preparation. Diverse educational purposes as well as diverse forms of preparation can and should be recognized even as standards are maintained. The College-Level Examination Program can help students gain this recognition. The unaffiliated and the transfer students who were formerly outside the mainstream are growing steadily in number. They present problems of counseling, placement, and accreditation that we have too long failed to solve. Satchel

91

Paige has said, "Don't look back—something may be gaining on you." We might add, innovation is still a mark of academic leadership. We can move ahead but it will take tenacious effort and time and a display of courage and, let it be said, some show of faith by the colleges. It seems evident that the best efforts of the College Board will not be effective unless institutions of higher education establish and implement policies and procedures whereby ambitious and deserving candidates can gain recognition of their achievement. It is important that the candidate who contemplates investing his time and money in the examinations do so with reasonable assurance that his achievement will be rewarded. Moreover, while candidates can accept rigorous examinations, they deserve to know that unreasonable standards have not been set.

We are not seeking to support cloistered virtue. We know that although it is difficult to study privately it is almost too much to ask that anyone do so and then come forward to be tested without clear encouragement that demonstrated achievement will be recognized.

The most troublesome problem the Program faces in its first stages of development revolves around the transfer student, for here the elements that combine in opposition are in part political and emotional. To oversimplify: the Program seeks, among other things, to facilitate the admission and placement of all transfer students; certain four-year colleges seek tests to help in the selection process; and the two-year colleges oppose the imposition of additional admissions barriers. The use of external examinations by institutions to which their graduates transfer is anathema to certain two-year college spokesmen. It is here that words like image, integrity, and discrimination are used, and it is here that the Program must demonstrate that it can help the transfer student who wants to go on.

The Council and the College Board staff believe that through the examinations the Program can provide positive assistance in the matter of transfer from two- to four-year colleges but that they should not be used as a substitute for procedures that are working. That is to say, first, that the transcript of courses taken and grades received during the two years at the two-year college should constitute the principal device by which admissions decisions are reached; second, that admissions requirements of four-year institutions should not be defined categorically and across the board but, rather, in individual cases wherever possible.

The Program could court a kind of chaos if it proceeded without the support of most of the two-year colleges. It hopes to earn this support

92

by doing everything it can to further the two premises cited above and by making clear through study that there are problems—counseling, placement, and articulation—that the College-Level Examination Program can help solve.

There are two kinds of students and two kinds of problems then that the Program faces at the outset. The problem that centers on the unaffiliated student is, basically, one of encouraging him, and this means establishing a workable system of credit by examination.

John W. Gardner, Secretary of Health, Education, and Welfare, has said: "Many people who study outside the formal system do so for reasons having to do with their own fulfillment, and care little for academic credit. Others are concerned only with the immediate acquisition of skills, and credit is irrelevant here too. But many others do wish to obtain academic credit. We shall serve these people far more effectively when we have devised a flexible system of credit by examination. Such a system would assess and certify accomplishment on the basis of present performance. The route that the individual had traveled to achieve competence would not come into question. Such a system would permit many individuals to participate in higher education who now—by nature of their jobs or other obligations—cannot do so. By 1970 many leading universities (and perhaps learned councils, state boards of education, etc.) should be offering credit by examination in standard academic subjects."[1]

In the effort to serve the transfer student, the problem is basically one of demonstrating to the two-year colleges that the Program will help, not hinder, access, placement, and counseling.

Both groups of students are large and growing larger. The problems they present are formidable, but are not the business of the students. They belong to those who would solve them, and the Board is prepared to make it easy for colleges to try.

Any institution that has not previously conducted a trial administration of the tests of the College-Level Examination Program may do so at no charge. The normal charges for the examinations are waived for these trial administrations, and the College Board provides scoring and score-reporting services.

This service is not limited to a single examination. An institution may arrange for a trial administration of one or several tests. Trial

---

1. "National Goals in Education," in *Goals for Americans*, by The American Assembly. Englewood Cliffs, N.J.: Prentice-Hall, Inc., 1960, pp. 94-95.

administrations of all examinations used need not be held at the same time. An institution may find it more suitable to conduct a trial administration of one examination in one semester and a different examination in a subsequent semester.

Obviously this service is intended to promote the use of the examinations where the college or university objectives and purposes and those of the Program seem to be compatible in the long run. The tests are not available under this arrangement to support individual research projects or projects primarily for institutional research that will not lead to continuing use of the Program. This is so because eventually the Program will be dependent on test fees. Requests for trial administrations will therefore be considered in the light of an institution's plans to make continuing use of the tests—that is, if the data from the trial administration demonstrates to the college that the tests are appropriate to the use intended. No institution need commit itself to long-range use of the tests in advance of a trial administration. However, an institution should consider how it would plan to participate in the Program and how this participation would be financed in the future, either by candidates or from institutional resources.

An institution wishing to conduct a free trial administration should communicate with the director of the College Board regional office in its area.

Daniel Burnham said "Make no little plans." We didn't. In this country our national goals and our essential needs for spiritual health are the same: to guard the rights of the individual; to insure his development; and to enlarge his opportunity. The sum of them is individual fulfillment. The chance to achieve it is what a democracy owes every citizen. And provided the chance, every man owes it to himself even more. Our deepest convictions impel us to cherish individual fulfillment, and I suppose that is what humanism is all about. It proclaims that puny as he is, man is the maker of his own destiny; he is touched with glory and in temporal things he is without limitation. What is the road? It is education. Ultimately, education serves all our purposes, individual and collective. It nurtures the vitality of our nation and sustains the aspirations of our soul. It does something else too; it serves as the key to equality of opportunity. Our quest for parity must always be coupled with two premises, first, we seek parity of *opportunity*, and second, individuals differ greatly in their aspirations and abilities. Someone once said there's nothing so unequal as the equal treatment of unequals.

94

What is almost too obvious to need saying is that each should be accorded respect and each should be able to work in his own style to his own top level. Diversity of purpose and preparation are not inimical to dignity, and no one has said it better than Mr. Gardner when he wrote of plumbers' pipes and philosophers' theories. The next step in respect for diversity of purpose and preparation is respect for diversity of educational programs, and it is here that a working system of credit by examination can be of tremendous use.

The Council on College-Level Examinations of the College Board believes that the traditional methods and present facilities of education just will not do; that the future calls for more education, and no end to education for all citizens; that flexibility, innovation, and independent study are essential in education; and, finally, that academic credit by examination is a key to this flexibility, innovation, and independent study. The Board therefore is staking a major effort in time, hope, and money to establish a national system of academic credit by examination, which I have described.

This Program is just starting. It won't solve everything, and it can't be perfect, but it can be the College Board's most important contribution to the welfare of higher education. If it fails, there's shame enough for all of us. But it won't, for despite our weaknesses and our anachronous dependence on rote and residence, insistence on access and opportunity is spreading. Moreover, there's a rare exhilaration in working hard to be, if not the very best we can, at least the cause of good in other men.

Recruiting the Disadvantaged: An Urgent Need[1]

Henry S. Dyer

At a College Board colloquium in 1955 I gave a talk in which one of my main points was that if college admissions was to become a valid part of the educational process, college admissions officers would have to stop acting like supersalesmen and make the recruiting of students more of a cooperative enterprise focused on the educational well-being of the student rather than on the financial well-being of the college.[2] After the talk was over, it was none other than Professor B. Alden Thresher who took me aside to give me some fatherly advice: he agreed with my general point of view but he thought I was being pretty unrealistic in supposing that college admissions officers could ever be converted from operators to cooperators.

Professor Thresher has since written a book that will become, in fact *is*, one of the really great classic statements on the role of college admissions in the nation at large.[3] After reading the book, I cannot believe that he still thinks college admissions officers are incapable of becoming cooperators. He himself, of course, is the living proof that true statesmanship in college admissions is a realizable possibility. In any case, I know his thinking and writing have had a very strong influence on me, and my own views owe much to his wisdom.

In speaking about college admissions for the disadvantaged, I am going to concentrate most of my attention on the most disadvantaged group in our society—the Negro Americans—and I am going to be focusing primarily on that aspect of college admissions that we call, for want of a better term, recruitment.

While preparing this paper I had occasion to ask an admissions officer in a predominantly Negro college to describe in some detail

1. This talk, given at the Colloquium on College Admissions Policies, Interlochen, Michigan, June 1967, is adapted from a paper delivered by the author at Howard University in April 1967, which was published in *The Journal of Negro Education* (Vol. XXXVI, No. 3, Summer 1967) under the title "Toward More Effective Recruitment and Selection of Negroes for College," pp. 216-229. Permission to reprint in this book has been granted by *The Journal of Negro Education*.

2. "Can College Admissions Be Part of Education?", *College Admissions: The Great Sorting*. New York: College Entrance Examination Board, 1955, pp. 43-50.

3. *College Admissions and the Public Interest*. New York: College Entrance Examination Board, 1966, 93 pp.

how he and his colleagues went about the work of recruiting students. During the course of the interview I made two interesting discoveries. The first was that the bush-beating techniques employed by that college today are but little different from those employed at the Ivy League colleges where my eyes were first opened to the realities of the college admissions business 25 years ago. The second discovery was perhaps somewhat more pertinent. As the conversation went on, it became apparent that my friend on the other side of the desk was becoming more and more uncomfortable about revealing the mysteries of his profession. He was being very gracious and frank, but obviously he was not altogether happy about the whole affair. I guessed what was wrong and suggested that maybe he felt that the recruiting of students was not quite educationally respectable. His reply was honest and prompt: student recruiting was *not* altogether respectable; it had to be done if the college was to have a reasonably able body of students— Negro *and* white—but it was nevertheless in the nature of things a sort of necessary evil.

A couple of weeks later I happened to find myself in intimate conversation with some admissions men who have been dealing at close range with the antics of coaches drumming up athletes to man the teams of some of the Big Name colleges in the East. This conversation also yielded two discoveries. The first was that the pressure to find top-notch athletes for college teams in the Ivy League is just as great today as it was in the good old days. And the second discovery was that these particular admissions officers took a dim view of the whole business as bordering on institutional hypocrisy, although they, too, for good and sufficient reasons, seemed to maintain the attitude that this kind of student recruiting, as indeed are most kinds, was probably a necessary evil.

I mention these two conversations in order to try to get this matter of student recruiting into the context of collegiate realities. There is recruiting and recruiting. It goes on practically everywhere all the time, and has been going on for a long time. It has various purposes, some of them rather cloudy, and not all of them primarily concerned with the betterment of students. Its methods are not always admirable, and at least some of the people who are closely engaged in the actual work have ambivalent feelings about the sort of system that seems to require it.

My main argument now—as in that earlier colloquium paper—is that college recruiting does not *have* to be a necessary evil or a form of institutional hypocrisy. It can be and should be seen as an entirely legitimate, in fact an indispensable, part of the total educational process by which a society makes the most of its people by helping them make the most of themselves. On the other hand, the uncomfortable feelings harbored by some sensitive people who are close enough to recruitment activities to know what is really going on ought to be a signal to all of us to take a hard look at those realities before taking off on flights of idealism about the more effective recruiting of Negroes and other disadvantaged students.

There is indeed plenty to deplore in college recruitment practices, past and present. The hard sell that lures some students into a type of education they may not be fitted for, or a type of college that is not sufficiently challenging for them; the appeal to middle-class snobbery; the use of scholarship funds to outbid rival colleges in the brain-and-brawn flesh market; the subtle techniques for getting high school counselors to steer their most attractive students to College A rather than College B—all such practices may seem to be well grounded in the American free enterprise system, but they hardly add up to a primary concern for the best interests of *all* youngsters who want and need some kind of education beyond the twelfth grade.

Before trying to figure out the most effective ways of getting more Negroes into college, I think we need to face up to some of the less publicized facts of the college admissions business and consider what it may be doing to students—all sorts of students, North and South, boys and girls, black and white.

About four years ago a group of colleges in the Middle West had the courage to take a look at themselves and their relations with the high schools around them.[4] The picture was not altogether pretty. The main outcome of the survey, as I read it, is that in the Middle West nobody on either side of the academic fence trusts anybody on the other side. And apparently most of this mutual suspicion is justified. "Most colleges," says the author of the survey, "reported that their admissions policy statements were *purposely* full of 'weasel' words" (emphasis added). Sixty out of 66 admissions directors said they knew of at least one high school principal who had lied about the qualifications of his students in order to get them into college. Half the high schools surveyed admitted that they sometimes withheld from the colleges "in-

---

4. Gordon A. Sabine, "Is There Static in the Education Channel?", *College Board Review* No. 51, Fall 1963, pp. 30-33.

formation they feel would jeopardize the student's chances for admission." In the light of these kinds of goings-on among those who run the so-called educational "system,"—that is, those who are supposed to be models of behavior to the upcoming generation—is it any wonder that a study of student honesty concludes with the disheartening estimate that by the time students reach college, half of them will admit to some form of academic dishonesty?[5]

A couple of years ago the New Jersey Association of Secondary School Administrators surveyed themselves and their guidance counselors to see what the colleges were doing to them.[6] This survey turned up "43 different bad practices," ranging over such matters as gross neglect of the academic and personal welfare of students once they have been impaled on the freshman roster, "lack of frankness or directness in talking with counselors about candidates and in talking with candidates themselves," "response to alumni pressure or political pressure and admitting clearly unqualified students without the school's endorsement," "subterfuge used with fellow professionals," concealing from candidates what it really costs to go to a given college, and so on.

Recruiters for predominantly Negro colleges have special difficulties. President Martin D. Jenkins of Morgan State College describes its unhappy experiences with high schools in an effort to develop a more integrated student body:[7]

"Major recruitment problems are presented by the large number of uncooperative counselors in racially integrated schools who make access to high school students difficult. In recently integrated schools, often the counselor fails to motivate Negro students to aspire for college and provides inadequate guidance to these students. So far we have found it virtually impossible to persuade counselors in the secondary schools of Maryland to present to white students the opportunities afforded by Morgan State."

It is reasonable to suppose that Morgan State College is not the only predominantly Negro college that is up against problems like these.

Earl McGrath in his classic study *The Predominantly Negro Col-*

5. W. J. Bowens, *Student Dishonesty and Its Control in College.* New York: Bureau of Applied Social Research, Columbia University, 1964. Mimeographed.
6. Robert L. Amsden, "Good and Bad Admissions Practices as Seen by High Schools," *Journal of the Association of College Admissions Counselors*, Vol. 11, No. 1, Summer 1965, pp. 3-6.
7. *The Morgan State College Program—An Adventure in Higher Education.* Baltimore: Morgan State College Press, 1964, p. 12.

leges and Universities in Transition[8] and Christopher Jencks and David Riesman in their more recent, and more controversial, article on the same subject[9] both point to a very special problem in the competitive recruitment of southern Negroes that can have serious consequences for all concerned unless it is faced with more candor than has hitherto been evident. The nub of the problem is this: the predominantly white colleges of the North, all well-heeled and many of them anxious to make a reputation for themselves as liberal color-blind institutions, have been moving into the South with ample scholarship funds during the last five or six years and creaming off the most highly qualified Negro students who would normally have gone to the Negro colleges of the South. This movement has had two effects on the southern Negro colleges. It has forced them to step up their own recruiting activities and driven them as a matter of self-preservation into taking boys and girls who might be better off elsewhere or not in college at all. It has also forced them to continue enrolling a disproportionate number of girls. There are complex ethical, social, and educational issues behind this North–South intercollegiate competition for Negro candidates—especially male candidates—which have not been faced by the involved institutions, North or South, and which *must* be faced if we are to avoid hurting further a good many people who have been hurt too much already.

It can be argued, of course, that competition is the life of trade, that it is the stimulus to excellence, that it is strictly in the American tradition, and all that sort of thing. One can reason that the more the colleges compete with one another for students, the greater the number of students who will find their way to college and the better off everybody will be. It is an argument not without some validity, but it can also be misleading, if not socially and educationally disastrous. In going along with it, we have to be careful that we are not merely rationalizing our meaningless institutional rivalries—rivalries that have little or nothing to do with meeting the developmental needs of students, whether they be in high school or in college or in transition between the two. I can hardly believe it does a youngster any good at age 17 or 18 to come to the stark realization that he is being used as a counter in a game of wits between his high school counselor and a bevy of college admissions officers, or between the rich university in the North and the

8. New York: Bureau of Publications, Teachers College, Columbia University, 1965, 204 pp.
9. Christopher Jencks and David Riesman, "The American Negro College," *Harvard Educational Review*, Vol. 37, No. 1, Winter 1967, pp. 3-60.

100

struggling little denominational college over in the next county in the South. Worse still, it probably doesn't do any youngster any good to realize that he is being left out of the game altogether and that in the blind shuffle that is supposed to separate the sheep from the goats he has wound up as one of the goats simply because he was a good deal less visible than Ralph Ellison's invisible man before *he* made it to college.[10]

The point I am trying to make is that student recruitment as usually conceived and practiced by colleges, whether they be mostly Negro or mostly white, is more likely than not to stand in the way of effective recruitment of Negroes, or of any other disadvantaged students, if one means by "effective recruitment" not just getting them into any college anywhere, but getting them into the most suitable college—one that will really give them a leg up in the kind of tough world they are going to have to cope with during the rest of their lives. And this is because the focus of the recruiters is usually too much on institutional prestige —on the needs of the institutions they serve—and not enough on the needs of the students whom the institutions are supposed to serve.

In the light of what I've been saying I should like to develop three themes: first, that the recruitment of Negroes for college does not *have* to be a function of institutional pride or self-preservation and that, if it is conceived broadly enough, it can be a powerful mechanism for bringing about important social change; second, that effective recruitment involves a great deal more than merely selling a youngster on the general notion that continuing his education is somehow "good for him," especially in the case of Negro boys and girls who have typically been cut off from normal educational opportunity and a chance to get some sense of what it might mean to live the good life; and third, that we need to become much more aware than we are now of what we do *not* know about the processes of recruitment and selection, and about the life problems of those whom we hope to recruit, if we are to achieve the kind of impact that is required by the enormous magnitude of the problem with which we are trying to deal.

In his essay on *College Admissions and the Public Interest*, Professor Thresher examines the college admissions process from three points of view, each more comprehensive than the one preceding. He first looks at the process from the standpoint of the individual student, second from that of the individual college, and third from that of the total complex

---

10. Ralph Ellison, *Invisible Man.* New York: Random House, 1952, 439 pp.

101

of schools, colleges, universities, and society at large. The central thesis of the book is that if college admissions is to be "in the public interest," it is this third level of complexity that must engage the attention of school guidance people, college admissions officers, and indeed all educators who are capable of thinking beyond the narrow confines of their own institutions. He describes this broadest approach to college admissions as "the 'systems' view of the entire process, . . . [It] involves the interaction of all the colleges and universities with each other and with secondary schools, as they appraise and deliver their annual crop of students coming forward out of society; it involves not only the 'manpower' demands of the economy in a narrow sense, but also the demands of the entire polity for an increasingly literate society, an increasingly knowledgeable electorate, and a citizenry with a depth of cultural awareness that would scarcely have been thought of a generation ago."[11]

When seen in light of the total social and educational system, the whole notion of student recruitment for college takes on a significance not usually attributed to it. When conducted "in the public interest," rather than in the interest of particular institutions, it becomes an activity having deeper purposes and employing methods that have only a coincidental resemblance to the competitive search for students with which we have become so familiar. Recruitment in this broader sense becomes one (but of course *only* one) of the important mechanisms by which we try to ensure that no one gets lost in the educational shuffle. It takes its place as part of the total effort to do something positive and constructive about the future of each individual and thereby helps to increase the likelihood that there will in fact *be* a future for the oncoming generation to inherit.

As a social process, then, the recruitment of students for college is one important means by which we should be able to reduce the fallout in our fragmented educational system. Frank Bowles speaks of the college admissions process as a "series of selections" that begins in the primary grades and ends when a student has found his niche either in a job or in some form of postsecondary education.[12] The selections are of two kinds. One kind consists of those that result from deliberate de-

---

11. Thresher, *op. cit.*, p. 26.
12. Frank Bowles, *Access to Higher Education: The International Study of University Admissions.* Paris: Unesco and the International Association of Universities, 1963, Vol. I, pp. 61-66.

102

cisions made by the student himself and his parents or by the educational institutions he attends or hopes to attend. The other kind of selection is that which results from "adventitious circumstances" that are outside the range of individual human choice or control: the social, cultural, and economic forces, the accidents of the environment, that help along the educational careers of some youngsters and cut short the careers of others. The purpose of student recruitment in its best sense is to minimize this second kind of selection so as to close the educational gap between the haves and the have-nots.

That a serious educational gap between whites and Negroes still exists is hardly a matter that needs rehearsing. If you are between the ages of 18 and 24, for instance, your chances of being in college or a professional school are two times greater if you are a white than if you are a Negro.[13] If you are a white adult, the chances are 50-50 that you have finished high school; if you are a Negro adult the chances are three-to-one that you have *not* finished high school.[14] If you are a young man coming up against the Armed Forces Qualification Test—a test that measures the basic skills you were supposed to have been taught in school—your chances of passing are 85 percent if you are white, only 36 percent if you are black.[15]

There is pretty general agreement that disparities like these are the result of remediable flaws in our educational and social processes, and of course it is at just these flaws that the recent education acts and the poverty programs have been aimed. But with all the money and the best will in the world the task of closing the gap is not going to be easy. A very considerable part of the difficulty of effecting change rests in the deeply ingrained beliefs many people still have about the mental development of children. The myth of the IQ and the immutability of human intelligence is still a powerful determinant in the ways children are taught, counseled, and classified.[16] Those who have abandoned this myth tend to come under the spell of another, namely, that the learning experiences a child has before the age of eight are so profound in their

13. Edwin D. Goldfield, *Statistical Abstract of the United States, 1966.* Washington, D.C.: Bureau of the Census, U.S. GPO, 1966, Tables 5 and 149.
14. *Ibid.,* Table 155.
15. Bernard D. Karpinos, "The Mental Qualifications of American Youths for Military Service and Its Relationship to Educational Attainment," pp. 92-99 in *Proceedings of the Social Statistics Section of the American Statistical Association, 1966.*
16. See, for instance, Orville G. Brim Jr., *et al., The Use of Standardized Ability Tests in American Schools and Their Impact on Students, Teachers, and Administrators.* New York: Russell Sage Foundation, 1965, pp. 134, 192-194.

effect that his mental growth pattern from then on is essentially un-changeable. There is good reason to think that a child's early learning experiences *do* have a strong influence on his later development,[17] but there is no real evidence that under appropriate instruction at least a good part of the early deficits cannot be made up. Project Head Start is all to the good for preschool children, but we cannot afford to wait 10 years for the graduates of Head Start to become candidates for college, for to do so would be to neglect some eight million disadvantaged children who were born too soon to get the benefit of the program. These are the six million white children and two million nonwhite children between grades 2 and 12 who come from urban and rural homes below the poverty line.[18] It seems to me this is the group that ought to be the prime target for an all-out college recruitment effort.

The suggestion that college recruitment should shift its principal focus from the most "promising" middle-class students in the last year of high school to the most disadvantaged pupils in both secondary *and* elementary school may seem like a radical if not a wholly unworkable idea. Perhaps it is. Nevertheless I believe it should be tried if for no other reason than to shake up our thinking about what the social function of college recruitment ought to be. I hope it underlines my main point — that college recruitment must get beyond narrow institutional concerns if it is to serve the broader purpose of helping disadvantaged and especially Negro youth surmount the educational, cultural, and social barriers that are keeping them back from their rightful place in the scheme of things.

At the turn of the century W. E. B. Dubois was quite right I think in urging greater concentration on the education of the Talented Tenth among Negroes.[19] But the situation is different now. Today the Talented Tenth of Negro youth are making it to college without much trouble — except for the pushing and hauling they get from the hordes of high-powered college recruiters who invade their high schools. The group that college recruitment needs to be much more concerned about is the Disadvantaged Four-Tenths of Negro youth who are caught in the urban ghettos and rural backwaters. I am not suggesting, of course, that college recruitment is the only way to get them out of there. Far

17. See Benjamin S. Bloom, *Stability and Change in Human Characteristics*. New York: John Wiley & Sons, 1964, 237 pp.
18. Goldfield, *op. cit.*, Tables 149 and 477.
19. E. Franklin Frazier, *Black Bourgeoisie*. New York: Collier Books, 1962, p. 62.

from it! But I do think that it can play an important role in the effort if it is seen as an integral part of the total complex of compensatory education. Skillfully done, it should help to bring the "presence" of college into elementary and secondary school classrooms early enough to become a live factor in opening up the horizons of youngsters for whom the future is a blank wall and the notion of college as a possible personal goal is nonexistent.

In Claude Brown's autobiographical novel, *Manchild in the Promised Land*, there is a poignant passage near the end that touches the heart of the situation:

"I had gotten my diploma from high school, and now I wasn't certain what I was going to do. I wanted to go to college, but it seemed like a dream. I didn't have any money. I didn't think I was good enough to get a scholarship from anywhere. There were a lot of things happening that made me sort of look at my desire to go to college as just one of those dreams that couldn't possibly come true."[20]

There have been a number of newly organized efforts to meet this problem. I shall discuss them presently, but I suspect that some of the most effective recruiting among the Negro disadvantaged—that is, of bringing the "presence" of college into their lives early and late—may often be of an informal character.

Recently I got to talking with a New York taxi driver who exemplifies in the finest way the possibilities in informal college recruiting. He was Negro, an émigré from North Carolina, with four children— two sons who had finished college, a daughter just about ready to graduate from one, and another son headed for college. This man gives practically all his free time to being a scoutmaster of a troop in Brooklyn and has been at this volunteer job for 15 years. His particular interest is in the Cub Scouts whom he teaches himself and whom he delights in following up as they move through the upper levels of scouting. He gets in touch with the parents when it looks as though a boy is going to quit the troop, keeps urging the boys on to make the most of themselves, and so holds before them some vision of their own possibilities for the future. Of course he loses some of his youngsters to the gangs; he told me that in his experience the critical period when this is likely to happen is around age 13. But he has had a lot of successes, too—kids who have stayed on, got to be Explorers, got into college if that seemed right for them, or if not, were on their way to some other

---

20. New York: The Macmillan Company, 1965, pp. 361-362.

decent future and productive life. This, I maintain, is one form of healthy college recruitment—of bringing the "presence" of the college as a symbol of an open future into the lives of youngsters at a time in their lives when it may have the best chance of making a real difference in their goals of life and in the likelihood that they will attain them. The world could do with a lot more people like that taxi driver from Brooklyn!

There's another moral to this story. It suggests that we can overdo all the grim talk about the disabilities of Negro youth to the point of talking ourselves into fruitless despair. Please do not misunderstand me. I do not underestimate the bitter and warping conditions that make the shaping of a career and a life so difficult for the children of the ghettos. The conditions are very real. In slum sections of New York City, for instance, it has been shown that the quality of the home situation is 85 percent accurate in predicting delinquency.[21] And Walter Daniel,[22] citing the unhappy comparison of lifetime earnings of nonwhite college graduates with those of white college graduates ($185,000 vs. $395,000), concludes, quite correctly, that such figures "contribute to the skepticism and despair that characterize a high percentage of Negro youth. Many express the attitude that training or retraining for job competence is futile." (It is this situation that explains, at least in part, the tendency of Negroes to reject the community college, as noted by Dr. Gleazer supra.)

My point is that, given all the discouraging predictions and all the hard and frustrating things Negroes have a right to be discouraged about, it seems to me that my taxi-driver-scoutmaster is nevertheless demonstrating in his own life and in the lives of many of the boys he is able to reach that one is more likely to overcome the tough realities if one simply refuses to be overwhelmed by them.

But, of course, we cannot depend on the random occurrence of dedicated taxi drivers to take us into the Promised Land. More effective recruiting of Negroes in the next five years and thereafter is going to have to depend on *well-organized programs of cooperative recruiting in depth* if it is to have the kind of widespread and immediate impact required to ameliorate the pressing problems of the students who are

21. Maude M. Craig and Thelma J. Glick, "Ten Years Experience with the Glueck Social Prediction Table," *Journal of Crime and Delinquency*, July 1963, p. 256.
22. "Needed: A Re-Examination of Plans for Disadvantaged Negro Youth," *The Journal of Negro Education*, Vol. xxxv, No. 3, Summer 1966, pp. 199-203.

now in the schools. How do things seem to be shaping up on this front?

Edmund W. Gordon and Doxey A. Wilkerson in their excellent and highly informative book, *Compensatory Education for the Disadvantaged*, have these encouraging words: "Current efforts to identify potentially able Negro and other socially disadvantaged youths and to help them go through college probably constitute one of the most dynamic trends in American higher education."[23]

On the basis of their extensive survey of all the colleges in the United States, they conclude that although the proportion of colleges engaging in some form of compensatory education is still pathetically small relative to the need, nevertheless many colleges "have accepted, at least in principle, the need for and the validity of special approaches to help socially disadvantaged young people to enter and succeed in college."[24] Their analysis shows that 38 percent of the colleges reporting some form of compensatory work had "practices addressed to helping disadvantaged students enter college [through] financial aid, modified admissions criteria, preparatory courses, and recruiting procedures. . ."[25]

There has been a considerable emphasis on special financial aid programs combined with intensive recruiting. Preeminent examples are the College Assistance Program, which links the National Scholarship Service and Fund for Negro Students (NSSFNS) with 110 colleges, and the National Achievement Scholarship Program for Negro Students, administered by the National Merit Scholarship Corporation. These programs tie adequate financial aid to the acceptance of disadvantaged students who are clearly academic risks. They are often also characterized by a *cooperative* effort on the part of the colleges to search out candidates who would not ordinarily think of applying to any college at all and would therefore be overlooked.[26]

These hunt-and-aid programs have a vital importance in the more effective recruitment of Negroes, but it seems to me that the most promising efforts to undo the injustices of the past are those that combine financial aid and recruiting procedures with a deep incursion into the *pre*college education of disadvantaged boys and girls. A considerable number of these have burgeoned in just the last four or five years:

---

23. New York: College Entrance Examination Board, 1966, p. 122.
24. *Ibid.*, p. 124.
25. *Ibid.*, p. 134.
26. *Ibid.*, pp. 136-138.

for example, The Yale Summer High School,[27] the ABC program at Dartmouth College,[28] Project Opportunity, sponsored by a group of 16 colleges in the South,[29] and the Rutgers Program in New Jersey.[30] All of these are aimed specifically at the likely college candidate early in his secondary school career, and at least two of them (Project Opportunity and the Rutgers Program) reach down as far as the seventh grade. All of the programs are so recent that it is still too early to decide which ones are on the right track and which ones are most likely to pay off in meeting the real educational needs of the young people involved in them.

The most massive effort at recruiting in depth is the Upward Bound program, which got under way only a couple of years ago under the auspices of the Office of Economic Opportunity.[31] This program currently involves 215 colleges, universities, and residential secondary schools all over the United States and its territories. It is serving 20,000 youngsters, most of whom have completed either the tenth or the eleventh grade.

There are three fundamentals in Upward Bound policy: (1) "thorough direct canvassing of the pockets of poverty in both urban and rural settings . . ." (2) a precollege instructional program that works intensively with the students during the summer and follows them up during the academic year from the tenth grade on, (3) cash allowances of $10 a week during each summer and $5 a week during the winter to help make up for the money these students would have earned on regular or part-time jobs. In short, it's a college preparatory program for the disadvantaged in which the colleges themselves are active participants.[32]

Richard Frost, the director of Upward Bound, estimates that there

---

27. Joel L. Fleishman, *Yale Summer High School: Report of the Director, 1965 Session.* Mimeographed.
28. Davis Jackson, *A Better Chance: An Educational Program Sponsored by Dartmouth College.* Mimeographed.
29. Darrell R. Morris, "Project Opportunity: A Status Report," *College Board Review* No. 61, Fall 1966, pp. 7-10, 30-31.
30. Gordon and Wilkerson, *op. cit.,* p. 141.
31. Richard T. Frost, *Upward Bound: Policy Guidelines and Application Instructions.* Washington, D.C.: Community Action Program, Office of Economic Opportunity, 1966.
32. The educational significance of Upward Bound, and other programs like it, may go well beyond its immediate objectives of helping the disadvantaged. It is introducing the colleges into secondary school instruction and counseling in a manner that could conceivably bring about desperately needed and revolutionary improvements in the educational process at both the college level and the secondary level.

108

are currently 600,000 high school youngsters who make up the total pool of disadvantaged young people of the type for whom the program is planned. In the summer of 1966, which was the first summer the program was in full operation, it enrolled about 3 percent of this disadvantaged 600,000.[33] The big question that begs for an answer is how the remaining 580,000 are to be found and served. This is a question that ought to lie heavy on the consciences of all the colleges—Negro and white—that are expending 90 percent or more of their recruiting strength in trying to beat their rivals to the best prepared brains in suburbia.

That recruitment programs like Upward Bound *can* do an effective job, if there is enough steam and imagination behind them, is strongly suggested by preliminary data on the pilot program that got under way with 953 students in the summer of 1965. Of these, 762, or 80 percent, actually went to college, and 370, or about 40 percent, were still enrolled last September.[34] In view of the fact that these figures come out of the first pilot experience with the program, before it had had a chance to get the effect of the recruiting-in-depth that is such an important feature, the 40 percent retention figure looks to me like a phenomenal achievement. Those 370 boys and girls who made it into the sophomore year are all pure gain for themselves and the society of which they are becoming a part. Had it not been for Upward Bound, practically none of them would ever have seen the inside of a college. It is reasonable to suppose that when we get more experience with this type of cooperative recruiting-in-depth, we shall get a better understanding of the process that will lead to even better results.

And this brings me to the final point I wish to emphasize in connection with more effective recruitment: we need to become much more aware than we now are of how much is *not* known about the processes of recruitment and selection and about the problems of life and outlook of those whom we hope to recruit. That is, we need to bring to the job some genuine intellectual humility as well as large amounts of energy, enthusiasm, and money.

To get into this aspect of the problem, I should like to touch briefly on the old problem of college entrance testing—a matter that has provoked not a little discussion among those concerned with estimating the probable college success of students from disadvantaged backgrounds.

---

33. According to a personal communication from Frost, dated March 1967.
34. *Ibid.*

109

It is a discussion with a long history laced with a considerable amount of mythology about what tests are capable or incapable of revealing about people and their possibilities. A recent phase of the discussion began when Kenneth Clark and Lawrence Plotkin published a study under the auspices of NSSFNS.[35] They concluded that the scores of the College Board Scholastic Aptitude Test (SAT) either fail altogether to predict the academic performance of Negroes at integrated colleges, or else *under*estimate the performance of Negroes as compared to whites. Studies by others, for example S. O. Roberts[36] and Julian Stanley,[37] have concluded that the same test when combined with high school grades shows as much predictive power in predominantly Negro colleges as in predominantly white colleges, possibly more. Last fall T. Anne Cleary analyzed entrance test data at three integrated colleges and found that in two of the colleges the predictive power of the SAT-high school grades combination was the same for Negroes and whites, while in the third it *over*estimated the college grades of Negroes as compared to those of whites.[38] And finally, Robert L. Linn[39] reanalyzed Cleary's data using the SAT alone as the predictor and got essentially the same results. Linn's speculations on their possible meaning are worth thinking about:

"It is of course possible that the Negroes tend to obtain higher test scores than their white counterparts with equal 'true' ability. I find this explanation extremely hard to believe. Unfortunately, a more realistic alternative explanation might be that instructors at the school tend to give lower grades to Negroes than to whites for the same performance. Another possibility might be that the Negroes . . . are not as well off financially as the whites and are required to hold more part-time jobs, thus leaving them less time to study."

In view of this mix of findings and speculations I think it is safe to

---

35. *The Negro Student at Integrated Colleges.* New York: National Scholarship Service and Fund for Negro Students, 1963, 59 pp.

36. *Studies in Identification of College Potential.* Nashville, Tenn.: Fisk University, 1962.

37. *Relative Predictability of Freshman Grade-Point Averages from SAT Scores in Negro and White Southern Colleges.* Madison: Laboratory of Experimental Design, University of Wisconsin, 1966. Mimeographed.

38. *Test Bias: Validity of the Scholastic Aptitude Test for Negro and White Students in Integrated Colleges,* College Entrance Examination Board Research and Development Reports, No. 18. Princeton: Educational Testing Service, 1966.

39. "Reanalysis of the Data of Miss Cleary's Predictive Bias Study." Princeton: Educational Testing Service, March 1967. Mimeographed memorandum.

110

conclude that the situation is somewhat confused and not altogether simple. But, as a tests and measurements man from way back, I am not ready to abandon the use of entrance tests like the SAT in sizing up college candidates—especially would I not abandon their use in the case of disadvantaged Negro candidates. What I would try very hard to get everybody in college admissions to abandon is the *mis*use of such tests.

I could carry on vehemently and at length about the psychometric superstitions that have bedeviled the educational enterprise for decades,[40] but that is another subject. The main point is this: the usual type of college entrance test gives a reasonably good indication of the basic skills in reasoning with words and numbers that a student has acquired presumably as a consequence of having gone to school. If he appears to be deficient in these skills and if we believe such skills are important for his success in college, then it seems to me of considerable importance for us to become aware of his deficiencies, *so that we can begin to take some specific action as early as possible to help him remedy the situation.* In view of how little we really know about cognitive functioning and development, it seems strange to suggest throwing away what little positive information we have in the form of test scores when such information might possibly help us in some small measure to accommodate our instruction to the needs of the individual. The trouble is that we have been so long accustomed to the idea that a student should be expected to conform to the academic demands of the college, that most of us are still having a hard time getting used to the notion that if a college is to educate—*really* educate—it must make its academic processes conform to the intellectual needs of the student insofar as we can understand them and appraise them.

But it is not only *intellectual* growth that most of us are interested in. We are also concerned that the student shall grow as a person, that he shall acquire some sense of who he is and where he is going in life and develop qualities like self-esteem and a decent respect for his fellowman. Here we are on even shakier psychometric ground. We call off the names of the characteristics we admire and hope for, but we hardly know what we mean by the words, and such measures of them as we have are extremely problematical, especially when we think of them in

---

40. For instance, my papers, "A Psychometrician Views Human Ability" (in *Teachers College Record*, Vol. 61, No. 7, April 1960, pp. 394-403) and "The Functions of Testing—Old and New" (in *Testing Responsibilities and Opportunities of State Education Agencies*; Albany: New York State Education Department, 1966, pp. 63-79).

the context of appraising students for college.[41] Yet we know in our bones that we must somehow take account of these so-called non-intellective factors if we are to do the right thing by those we propose to teach. Kenneth Clark said it well in an earlier colloquium: we must (he said) "concern ourselves with [the] subtle and complicated factors which seem to be operative in blocking the academic potential of children of stigmatized or rejected groups. Systematic studies of the psychosocial development of these [disadvantaged] children reveal that quite early in their lives . . . they are burdened with conflicts and ambivalence about self, feelings of inferiority, and, at times, self-hatred. . . . The educational implications of this inner turmoil should not be too difficult to perceive and study. Burdened as they are by these feelings of inferiority and crucial ego conflicts and the necessity to develop protective patterns of behavior, it becomes understandable why so many of these children seem psychologically unable to profit from a normal school experience. It would seem that schools could compensate for the psychological burdens of these children by understanding the nature and basis of the problem; . . ."[42]

But such understanding has been slow in coming. A study by David E. Hunt and Robert H. Hardt, *Characterization of 1966 Summer Upward Bound Programs*, makes a beginning at showing how the experience may have affected these deeper personal characteristics, but the outcomes are still only a beginning.[43] Like most researchers in this hard-to-master domain they urge caution in the interpretation of their findings and hope for "in depth" interviews of the students to get better clues as to what kinds of effects the program is having on what kinds of students.

Another study that seems to me likely to bear good fruit in helping us understand better what the Negro adolescent boy is up against is the so-called Pathways Project, which is just entering its second year in Boston.[44] This is a series of "in depth" case studies extending over the whole adolescent period. It will try to find out what factors in the home,

41. Samuel Messick, "Personality Measurement and College Performance," pp. 110-129 in *Proceedings of the 1963 Invitational Conference on Testing Problems*. Princeton: Educational Testing Service, 1963.
42. "Disadvantaged Students and Discrimination" in *The Search for Talent, College Admissions* 7. New York: College Entrance Examination Board, 1960, p. 17.
43. Syracuse, N.Y.: Syracuse Youth Development Center, 1967.
44. Robert A. Rosenthal, *et al.*, *Pathways Project: Progress Report, 1965-1966*. Cambridge, Mass.: Harvard Graduate School of Education. Mimeographed.

the school, and the community are most important to each individual as he copes with the people around him in trying to find a pathway out of the ghetto. The enormous importance of such studies to any college recruitment program should be obvious: only as college recruiters are informed in depth and in detail about the personal and social needs of the individual youngsters they seek will they be successful in helping them find a pathway into adult society. We have been too content too long with describing these students in the mass with a few numbers derived from tests. We must now learn how to see each one as an individual person engaged in his own peculiar problems and in a search for goals that will make life meaningful for him.

The situation can be summed up with five major propositions:

1. The recruitment and selection of Negroes and other disadvantaged students for college is an indispensable part of the total educational process by which American society attempts to make the most of all its people by helping all of them make the most of themselves.

2. The effectiveness of this recruitment process is currently being hindered by a form of intercollegiate competition for candidates that is too much motivated by purely institutional considerations and not enough by consideration of the needs of the students themselves.

3. To make the recruitment process effective in closing the educational gap between Negroes and whites, we must shift our primary focus away from Dubois' Talented Tenth and direct a much greater part of our effort toward the Disadvantaged Four-Tenths.

4. To move in this direction with the swiftness required by the urgency of the situation, we cannot depend only on the random recruiting efforts of dedicated individuals (although these are extremely important); we must mobilize our resources in well-organized programs of cooperative recruiting-in-depth.

5. Such programs as Upward Bound show that cooperative recruiting-in-depth is both possible and effective, but they also demonstrate that the effort must be enormously increased if it is to be adequate to the need and that we still have much to learn if we are to become maximally effective in helping Negro boys and girls find their way out of the ghetto.

Harold R. Isaacs, writing in the Spring 1967 issue of *Daedalus*,[45] made a penetrating observation about the role of color and physical

45. "Group Identity and Political Change: The Role of Color and Physical Characteristics," pp. 353-375.

113

characteristics in our culture. He emphasized that, "The gap [between Negroes and whites] is not economic alone. The habits of mind created by this long history of mastery and subjection are part of the culture itself in all its many manifestations. Conscious and unremitting effort will be needed to free the culture of the many gross and subtle ways in which it has shaped whites and non-whites to these patterns. This effort begins in the political, legal, and economic systems, *but then must move into society's educational systems and religious establishments.*" [Emphasis added.]

In short, the number one problem of our time is right in our own hands. We cannot afford to fumble it.

114

On the University, Admissions, and International Education

Albert G. Sims

Coming as I do from a career in international affairs and education in government, in the Institute of International Education, and, more recently, in the College Board, I would like to try to give a view, in some perspective, of the university (meaning higher education) both historically and in its international setting and to relate this view to the function of admissions and to certain more important problems in respect to foreign student admissions. I have approached this task without attempting to rival, with words, the style of Frank Lloyd Wright, the elegance of Edward Everett Stone, the grandeur of Le Corbusier, or even the stark functionalism of Harrison and Abramovitz. Rather, as with the rooms in Habitat at Expo '67, I have simply collected some thoughts in a single structure to suit the convenience of the builder and spark the curiosity of the user. There is no pretense to symmetry in the outcome. I am well aware of the vulnerability of my generalizations. They are meant to be a set of impressions that it is hoped will stimulate admissions officers to insights about the essential nature of the admissions function in the university and the problem of foreign students.

It is both comfort and refuge, in the flux of change, to honor ancient myths. One of these myths is that the university is, and in nobler forms has always been, an institution unique for its autonomy and for the sanctuary it affords in society for the free pursuit of knowledge and learning associated with its acquisition. According to this idea, those who seek entry to the university community are judged simply for the seriousness of their purpose and the quality of their talent for these pursuits. Once admitted, they share a shelter from the pressures and passions of the outside world in the company of students and scholars at universities everywhere.

What is comforting about this static and lofty model, especially for admissions officers, is that it makes the function of university admissions straightforward and simple. They are concerned with talent for scholarship and purposefulness. They are not concerned with the foreign student, the in-state student, the out-of-state, the child of an alumnus, an underprivileged student . . . nay, even the athlete and the nonathlete, as different units of quantitative measurement in the admissions process.

115

Alas, the myth disintegrates in the telling, and the comfort is illusory. No need to belabor the argument with the massive evidence of how forces outside the university—the public generally; the federal, state, and local governments; the foundations; and business and industry— are all shaping its character, style, and scope. The myth is too patently unreal to persist as a useful part of the folklore. The myth is dead.

But if the myth once useful is now dead, what is the real situation with the university? Or what is the currently relevant mythology? Is the university an amorphous thing to be buffered and shaped by all the external forces exerted upon it? If indeed it is, this fact too should be known because of the implications it would have for the admissions functions.

Now admissions officers may say, "We have no need for a theory, a hypothesis, or a myth about the university to know our admissions functions. We know the texture of that function very well and quite pragmatically from our daily encounter with the job." No one can deny the knowledge derived from the daily encounter. But it is precisely at this point that I would rise to challenge the admissions people. Can they sensibly relate what they are doing to the nature and central purposes of the university and to the relationships of the university to the larger community? If they cannot do this—not only to their satisfaction, but to that of the university as a whole and the public that supports it—then they cannot claim mastery of the job and in fact the job may be mastering them.

These, then, are the questions I address: What *is* the university (and higher education) in relation to the larger community? Does it have an essential character that determines, or ought to determine, its responses to the larger community? And how does all of this relate to those who have responsibility for access to the university? Finally, what do these responsibilities have to do with foreign student admissions? Anyone who thinks that this is a large order comes equipped with the perception necessary for the task.

I shall begin by making some very general observations about the history and evolution of the university in the Western world, and from these observations, draw conclusions that seem to have relevance to an understanding of the role of the university and its relationship to the society in which it exists. I shall then attempt to infer from these conclusions their more particular significance from the standpoint of the admission of students, generally, and foreign students, especially.

The earliest of the Western universities—such as Bologna, Paris,

116

Oxford, Cambridge, Salamanca, and Prague—emerged in the twelfth and thirteenth centuries from the structure of education within the Church. (Some believe, it is curious to note, that the university at Oxford was founded by foreign—English—students and scholars expelled from the university in Paris in 1167 as a result of the tension between the two countries.) In particular, these earliest universities were licensed and their degree-granting authority was conferred by the state or Church. Their existence, growth, and multiplication reflected the fact, first, that the Church itself could no longer wholly meet its need to evolve and communicate its dialectic and law for its community and, second, that the growth of secular authority required its own base for the development of law, medicine, and the arts.

From such beginnings, the Western university nestled uneasily from time to time between the competing authorities of Church and state. Usually, it was the center for conservatism. But occasionally, as in the Reformation, it became the hot anvil for shaping great new movements. Not infrequently, such as in the early nineteenth century in Germany and the twentieth century in Poland, the Low Countries, and Norway, the universities were casualties of war and politics.

The Western university came into being as an institution by act of the most powerful authorities in the society to meet needs that were generated by, or were at least important to, these authorities. In the eight centuries of their existence, the universities have been quiet sanctuaries only when they have been insignificant and fallow. When they have been at the high tides of their influence, they have been engaged in the great issues of their day. This is a perception essential to any understanding of the role of the university.

The Christendom of Western Europe, especially during the medieval period, did provide a more or less homogeneous community within which students and scholars could move with relative freedom to distant universities. This movement resulted in the main from the attraction exerted by distinguished chairs upon scholars throughout the area. The impelling force creating this movement was the individual's desire to share in the quality of learning as he could identify it through the reputation of great scholars. Sometimes, apparently, the king or bishop had to extend a hand of protection against the local burghers to the "foreigners" thus aggregated around the university. This presumably is the ancient origin of the perennial town-and-gown problem. But, regrettably, sanctuary of this kind for the university—by courtesy of the sovereign's rights—has disappeared.

117

In the nineteenth century, similar forces of attraction resulted in the movement of students from East Asia to the United States and American students to the German universities. There was a difference, however. Generally, Orientals came to the United States and Americans went to Germany because of the reputation of the universities visited and the presumed qualities of the countries these universities served, rather than for the commanding presence of individual great teachers. The movement, moreover, was recognizably "international," whereas the distinguished Scotsman of the fifteenth century who with honor left St. Andrews for a chair at Bologna would never have surmised that he was part of an "international educational exchange program." Here, in the nineteenth-century movement of students to foreign countries, can be perceived first traces of the influence of the developing nation-state in the commerce of education.

From these observations, several conclusions may be reached. One is that the "universality" of the early and medieval university perhaps reflected not so much its "international" character as its existence within a culture (Western Europe) of somewhat common consistency. It was a culture in which secular power felt less need for constraint in the movement of students and scholars than the Church and the professions had for the freedom of movement. Another conclusion might be that from the beginning of what is now known as international education exchange, a central motivation of students in this movement has been their desire for experience in a university setting made especially attractive because of the attributes or reputation of the society in which the university exists. Differently stated, students began to come to the United States and to go abroad because of aspirations for a kind of knowledge that would presumably advance their own interests and those of their own society in achieving "a better life."

Governmental recognition of education and "culture" as national assets and instruments of foreign policy first became conspicuous in the years before World War II. The Latin American Good Neighbor Policy of the Roosevelt administration featured such recognition, and the creation of the Office of Cultural Relations in the Department of State in 1938 institutionalized it. In the aftermath of the War, "education and cultural relations" became adapted to a variety of national purposes: to reorient the occupied people; to display the essential nature and the attainments of the United States as a means of getting sympathy and, it was hoped, international understanding; to promote special communities of interest, as with Western Europe; to help with

118

institution-building and national development abroad and so promote this country's security; and so forth.

With notable lack of theory, design, or coordinated impulse, the federal government has made progressively more "use" of education as an ingredient of foreign policy operations during these past 20 years. The word "use" is deliberately chosen. The universities have had little to do with the policy development. Most federal funding has been in the form of service purchases from the universities, with specifications supplied. Little support has been in the unrestricted form of general subsidy to enable the universities to strengthen the international aspects of their education programs.

From this last set of observations, a tempting assortment of conclusions are possible. Mine are as follows:

1. Within the last three decades education, especially higher education, has been increasingly associated with national security. The federal government, as well as governments in other countries, has, as a result, exhibited a growing concern and aggressive initiative with respect to the character of education, its quality and extensiveness, and the uses to which it is put. This concern and this initiative have generally been manifest as a force working on education, rather than within it or even in partnership with it.

2. Education has been identified as a major instrumentality, for the ordered and orderly change necessary to meet the increasing pressures around the world generated by this revolution in consumer expectations. Education is thought to be a principal means of closing the growing gap between the nations of the north and south, between the rich and the poor, between (if you will) the United States and all the rest. The gap is presumed to be dangerous because it induces international tensions and conflict. It will be recognized that this is a special instance of concern with education as an aspect of national security.

3. In the face of this concern and initiative, the universities have demonstrated little capacity to rationalize their interests and assert them with unified voice and collective authority. In point of fact, the impact of these outside forces on the universities has tended to weaken their vigor and integrity as institutions representing centers of educational leadership. With the lure of government contracts, foundation grants, and the interests of their professional associations through which their mobility and their access to these resources are enhanced, faculty has become largely "other oriented."

4. Paradoxically, universities have become both more parochial and

119

more universal in nature. They have become more parochial in the sense that in each country they are more or less conjoined with pre-university education in a common system. Since preuniversity, or perhaps more accurately "preprofessional," education differs substantially by country in content, access, and purpose (and will continue to do so as long as there are important differences in culture, national aims, and capabilities among countries), the university components of these national systems differ. The first years of the university system are apt to reflect these differences in greatest degree. On the other hand universities at the level of specialization tend to be somewhat similar, particularly in the sciences, because of their common concerns and rapid communication.

5. The United States government initiative with respect to international education, the consequences of its post-World War II role of leadership in international affairs, and affluence and ease of mobility have all been factors in creating a widespread demand for an educational experience abroad by this country's university students.

These, then, are the observations and related conclusions (it would be more modest to say "assertions") that are to be the basis for some inferences about the role of the universities, their relationship to the outside world, and, in particular, admissions and international education. The conclusions stated lead more easily and meaningfully to such inferences if they are taken as a whole rather than individually, and this will be my procedure.

I turn once again to the role of the universities and suggest that their history makes evident their natural and substantial involvement in their contemporary society. There is no valid issue, per se, of their defense as sanctuaries against the encroachment or influence of the world outside the universities. Nevertheless, such an issue has developed and persisted with the universities in Latin America. It is here that the idea of "university autonomy" has been made a critical political issue. This is a special phenomenon having much to do with the caudillo character of Latin American governments in recent history, the alienation of Latin American universities from the governmental power structure, and the consequent unique political function of the university in that area. Whatever the special circumstances, a good argument can be made that the Latin American concept of university autonomy has tended to isolate the universities from their natural responsibilities in their societies and to depreciate their quality as educational institutions.

120

For the central problem of the modern university is relevance, not autonomy. Relevance is an imperative not only as an interior concern of the university for the quality of its educational function but as a demand of growing insistence upon the university by the community. The educational community is aware of this. The connections between the university and the world around it have always been vital, but what is different in these last decades is that these connections have become greatly extended, overwhelmingly apparent, and utterly crucial. The equilibrium of modern society depends on science, technology, and (if the phrase may be forgiven) human engineering. These are the fields, historically and inevitably, of concern to the university.

If this is so, is the relevance of the university thereby to be taken for granted? The answer is quite clearly "no." Some critics, and they are not all students, do seriously challenge the relevance of the modern American university, as we know. The problem is that though the case for relevance is more apparent, the achievement of it is progressively more complex and difficult, taxing the university for extraordinary qualities of flexibility.

To make the point we have only to examine further what is meant by "relevance." What is in fact involved is a highly differentiated set of community needs and institutional responses in the field of higher education. No longer is "the university" a meaningful definition of institutional organization, purpose, and function in this context. In the totality of this interaction between community and higher education, each institution has the particular responsibility of differentiating its role. No institution, even the emergent "multi-university," can realistically aspire to span all needs in higher education. The institutional differences of which I speak are more pervasive than the nomenclature suggests: the two-year or junior college, the liberal arts college, the university. The universities of California, Michigan, Harvard, and Minnesota have quite different roles to play as educational institutions. This is both necessary and inevitable. The significant question is: what factors in each case determine relevance and role and how is the university equipped to act in continuous perception of the requirements of relevance?

The requirements of relevance do not all stem from outside the university, of course. In an important sense, the first test of relevance is met within the university itself: do students and faculty share a sense of being in the "real world" and do students in particular perceive that they are engaged in both a social and learning experience that is mean-

121

ingful and connective? The imperatives demanding relevance from out-side the university have their reflections within the university. The images in the reflections may not be the same—the student will always to a degree be embattled against the "establishment"—but this only complicates the task of the university. This point should not be passed lightly. The complication can in fact be fatal for the university. Its mission as intermediary between the generations in times of the rapid shift and drift of values becomes what may be its most important re-sponsibility.

The recent experience of the universities with the federal govern-ment in the business of international education is, I believe, an object lesson for the universities. The message, or the object of the lesson, I would put in this form: when requirements outside the universities arise for new or expanded university involvement and the universities themselves do not respond adequately, the terms of their response will be determined by the external authority (or government) using funds to command their resources. The message is oversimplified, but essen-tially true.

Although the university should be relevant and responsive, it must never be subservient. It has the task in any society of marshaling the best resources available to it for investigation and communication con-cerning the total needs of the society and the condition of man in it. The university has an integrative role; it cannot be "had" by any single group, even the government from which it may get its principal sup-port and authority for existence.

If admissions officers conceive the admissions responsibility in the university as that of processing applications efficiently with minimum public disturbance they will have deserted this Habitat early in its con-struction. If, on the other hand, they are still with me, they will surely agree that the admissions responsibility is more than technical and that the role and relevance of the university is significantly shaped by, and expressed through, admissions policy. In the admissions office is what is perhaps the most current and pertinent intelligence of the university bearing on its concerns for its role and relevance. And there that in-telligence will stay, unused and unexploited, unless the admissions director perceives the breadth of his role and its vital relationship to institutional policies. Moreover, it is not only that he must be percep-tive about the uses of his own intelligence. He must also have aware-ness of the intelligence of others in the university for its pertinence to his responsibility. The tone and tensions within the university's student

122

body, for example, represent critical feedback for him and for admissions policies.

Earlier I made reference to international education, taking it as an object lesson for the universities. Having criticized the universities for a failure of initiative in this instance, I can fairly be held to account for what they should now do in this field of their interests. The inventory of things to be done is extensive, but it can be restricted for this purpose to a consideration of one important item—the case of foreign undergraduate students.

The "brain-drain" seizure, which will apparently continue to afflict us, has already had one important side effect. It has substantially deepened the doubt about the wisdom of foreign student exchanges at the undergraduate level and it has visibly reduced the disposition to promote such exchanges. We all know the kind of consensus that seems to have developed as an expression of such doubts. The foreign undergraduate comes at the more impressionable age, stays longer, gets more involved in the campus as a community and in American life generally —and in this process becomes alienated from his home culture. In any event, he is the more likely to remain in the United States. Some people may say that this is not bad and that it is only a special phenomenon of the type to which this country owes its origins and growth.

Whether or not a consensus exists, we need not now debate this issue. We need only accept the fact that support for foreign undergraduate students *is* diminishing because the sources of funds for the purpose in the United States are drying up and because countries abroad are more and more imposing restraints on study abroad at this level. Both these circumstances have had direct consequences for the well known and respected African Scholarship Program of American Universities (ASPAU), which has fallen in volume to about one-third that of its earlier years. This is a program oragnized by, and specifically for, the colleges and universities. It successfully pioneered new and improved techniques for foreign student selection. It represented a cooperative college enterprise joined to substantial governmental interests. Yet for all this, it has come to a dead end.

Why? Are the interests of the colleges in foreign undergraduates at fundamental variance with those of governments—United States and foreign? Or is it simply that the colleges, grown accustomed to government and other outside support for foreign undergraduates, have an unfulfilled responsibility in this matter? Not so in either instance, I suggest.

123

If the strength and vitality of undergraduate education in this country are improved by the presence of well selected foreign students, it is in the general interest of institutions to assure the presence of such students. And if it is important to the quality of these institutions, it can be demonstrated to be in the national interest, worthy of governmental support. (This may sound like, but is not, an application of "auto" Charley Wilson's law: "What's good for GM is good for the country." Anyone who cannot perceive the difference should ask himself why he's in education.)

The case in these terms for governmental support of foreign undergraduate programs is plausible enough, but has had little recognition in government circles. Governmental support for educational exchanges has so far been justified mainly in relation to foreign policy objectives: reorientation, international understanding, international development, and so forth. *It has not been justified as support for the country's education, and educators have failed to make the point cogently on these grounds.*

There is little hope of being persuasive with this point if strengthening the programs of the colleges in this way would in the process conflict with other government objectives, such as those mentioned above. But conflict is not inevitable. Governments fear manpower losses in such exchanges; colleges want foreign students. If colleges can design foreign-student opportunities minimizing the possibilities of manpower losses (preferably cooperatively with foreign institutions, which are likewise concerned with student manpower distribution), undergraduate exchange can be made feasible. A key to an imaginative solution of the problem by the colleges may be in the realization that programs for United States students abroad and for foreign students can be usefully interrelated, both in purpose and in execution.

More specifically, I would propose that:

1. Foreign undergraduates be accepted, generally, at the third year undergraduate level and no lower; this will usually mean at least a year or two at a university at home.

2. The stay of the foreign student, at this level, be generally not more than one year.

3. His program be specially designed to the extent necessary to provide him a year that counts in his home university program.

4. Insofar as possible these special programs for foreign undergraduates be part of reciprocal arrangements with foreign universities on behalf of United States students.

124

In the beginning, I said there would be no symmetry, but there has been a certain unity intended. Its theme could be traced in the following terms.

The university has always been involved with the "public interest" of its times. The rise of nationalism in its nineteenth- and twentieth-century form created the setting for what are now known as "international education and cultural exchanges." The country's national interest in higher education in recent decades was first expressed in relation to foreign policy purposes. This interest included no particular concern for the condition of educational institutions, but rather for what they could contribute to the achievement of the government's objectives. In their response the universities did not distinguish themselves. They did not much advance their interests and in fact lost some of their cohesion and strength. Later, the focus of national interest in education shifted to more urgent grounds, military security (in the National Defense Education Act), then still later, to the broader base of education as national resource and sinew of strength, economic and political as well as military.

More than ever the university is involved with the public interest. Its record with the deepening of this involvement is not impressive. The admissions function has great potential for helping develop the creative initiative and response necessary from the universities if they are to be more than merchandizing houses. The case of the foreign student is in point. The capacity to perceive and integrate the interests of the community (including governments) and education is called for; is educational statesmanship of this order available? It is everywhere needed by those who manage the universities' interests.

Campus Environment as a
Factor in Admissions

Theodore M. Newcomb

I would like to describe briefly a pair of studies I did at Bennington College 25 years apart. Somewhat to my surprise, some of my findings in these studies demanded, for interpretation, an understanding of the student selection process that went on.

I want to say something about self-selection, the image of a college, and the program or programs of a college, and the interdependence of these three things. Then, something about strategy for changing both selection and program, presumably changing them together as they're related to one another in a changing world. A couple of memorable sentences in a memorable book I read a good many years ago appear in G. G. Simpson's *The Meaning of Evolution*.[1] In the midst of a discussion of evolution, these sentences suddenly leap out of the page at the reader. "No one knows how dinosaurs became extinct. We know only that something changed, and dinosaurs did not." Maybe some universities have something in common with dinosaurs—in size at any rate. We can only hope we won't follow them into extinction.

Now for the two studies done at Bennington College, the first one in the late thirties,[2] the second one in the early 1960s.[3] The students selected themselves in very different ways at this same institution at these two different times, and I want to talk about the major findings, in order to relate this fact to admissions. The college opened in 1932. It was a brand new institution for women. It was isolated in the Green Mountains of Vermont. It was a very expensive place, for the interesting reason that, when its founders had almost got their buildings put up, they lost all their money in the Depression. The question was, do we go out of business with our buildings up, or do we find some other way of financing ourselves? They decided on a policy that they have more or less maintained to this date. Namely, first, drawing up a budget of what they would need; second, estimating the number of students

---

1. New Haven: Yale University Press, 1950, 364 pp.
2. *Personality and Social Change.* New York: Holt, Rinehart & Winston, Inc., 1943, 225 pp.
3. *Persistence and Change: Bennington College and Its Students after Twenty-five Years.* New York: John Wiley & Sons, Inc., 1967, 292 pp. (With K. Koenig, R. Flacks, and D. Warwick.)

who would be there; third, dividing the first by the second—and this becomes the fee that will be charged. At first, 100 percent of their revenue came from students' fees. For the first few years, correcting for inflation since 1932, it cost the students the current equivalent of nearly $5,000 a year; this cost, as might be guessed, had something to do with selection processes of students.

In the late thirties I began a four-year follow-up study at Bennington, because I hadn't been there as much as a year when it was clear to me that it was not like any other institution I had known. Something was gripping students. They showed a kind of cohesiveness and sense of vivid community life that I wanted to study. I didn't know whether it was because it was small, because it was new, or what. I wasn't even sure what the content of it was that held them together. These were the things I wanted to find out.

I had a good deal of information on every student who entered the college during the four years. There were only 250 students at the time. Some pretesting showed that the ways in which the students changed most, even during a year, and quite generally within two years or more, was in terms of the then-existing scene of public affairs. In case there are some people who don't remember, or never heard their grandfathers tell, what things were like during the great American Depression, it really occurred, and it really had effects, and there was very little on the public scene that wasn't affected by it.

The faculty at Bennington were mostly very young. I left the college before I was 40, and I was one of the older people on the faculty. This faculty, most of whom were newly out of universities, in Depression times, became concerned when it was discovered that we were going to have to take mostly girls from "very select" finishing schools in the East, because they were almost the only ones who could afford to pay, and they came mainly from very respectable families. Before the students had been there very long, the faculty had to come to the semispoken, or hardly-spoken, conclusion that one of our tasks was to see to it that these students learned something about the other half of the world—or should I say the other 99 percent of the world—from which they had been pretty much secluded; in fact, they had almost no notion of what was there. They knew much more about what was happening in Europe—these were the days of gathering war clouds—than they did about the effects of the Depression in their own country, we sometimes felt. But at any rate, the faculty was self-conscious about bringing them out of their seclusion. One consequence of this, which was not very

127

difficult to discern after my studies had gone on for a little while, was that there was a regular and steady drift away from what would have then been called a conservative attitude toward the dominant position of the American public in the 1930s, which could best be described, I suppose, as in support of "The New Deal." The great majority of students changed—many of them quite conspicuously. That wasn't why I made the study. It was generally known before I made the study. The question was, what kinds of students, under what kinds of conditions, did and did not change in this direction? Since I devoted most of a book to answering this question, I can't possibly do more than summarize ever so briefly here. It comes out quite clearly as follows: those students who were the most deeply involved in the institution, who were active and loyal to the college, who took it seriously, who were respected and looked up to by their fellow students, were the ones who showed the most change.

This was a bit dramatic, as of then, because at most colleges the students who were respected and held a position of trust and were looked up to by others were not those who were veering toward the radical. In fact, it was just the other way. Those who were suspected of radical positions typically were not those who were considered the solid citizens of the community.

I was interested in the fact that at this college things differed a good deal from Williams, just over a mountain, which I also studied as a kind of a control group. By and large, many Williams boys came from the same families, at least the same communities, as did the Bennington girls. At Williams I found rather noticeable changes in attitudes toward public issues, but primarily in only two departments, economics and political science. Apart from that there was little or no change at Williams from freshman to senior year. At Bennington, it wasn't that way. Whether or not students changed their attitude, as the majority did, wasn't a function of what department they were in. It was a function of how deeply involved they got with the community as a whole. And this could be shown in ever so many ways. It happened to modern dance majors and it happened to physics majors—and literature majors and social science majors. It was quite clearly a function of the community as a whole.

This happened as a complex interaction-effect of a lot of things. The college was new and there was a good deal of pride in getting into an institution just started. It had a very special educational philosophy. In those days it probably would have been called, and certainly was

128

called in some quarters, a venture in progressive education. The college was isolated. Typically, our students left the campus two weekends out of a term, which meant they were on this Green Mountain hilltop most of the time. They had a very actively participating faculty and all kinds of activities involving the entire community, with relatively little separation between students and faculty. Most of all, perhaps, was the fact of the times. People were concerned about public issues, both at home and abroad. And, as I will indicate more fully later, the manner in which they had to be selected, given the circumstances, had something to do, I believe, with their rather conspicuous attitude changes.

The follow-up study done 25 years later had two parts. The first was a restudy of all the individuals who took part in the earlier one. By now, they were widely scattered. Several of them were grandmothers, and quite a number of their daughters were now at the college. I was interested in finding out what had happened to these people—especially to those who had, during their four years in college, gone through a good deal of fairly substantial attitude change.

I can answer that question rather quickly.

Some hundreds of girls, relatively affluent and previously "protected," came quite innocently to a college that they expected to be respectable—after all, it was sponsored by prestigious people—and when they got there, they found, before the four years were over, that they were on the opposite sides of many fences from their parents. They had changed quite a lot, as indicated in many ways. What had happened to them after 25 years? The typical response, when I ask people to guess, is, "Well, these girls will be married, and they'll be married to men of their own kinds, which means they will go back to their own community, or a community just like it, and naturally there will be a good deal of regression; while some of them will have been, so to speak, converted, and will hang onto it, most of them will become somewhat like the conservative husbands to whom they are married." This was the general prediction, though by no means the universal one. Here are the facts: there was practically no regression, that is, going back to their freshman attitudes. There was even some progression or extension toward even less conservative attitudes.

But I was not merely interested in the fact that there wasn't very much regression. I was interested in the conditions under which it did or did not occur. What kinds of individuals, under what kinds of conditions, maintained or even extended their attitude changes? What kinds did not? Again, I must summarize quickly. (By the way, we got in touch with these students 25 years after they graduated by choosing graduates of three consecutive classes for consecutive study and simply going where they were. We got to something like 94 percent of the living graduates for whom we had names and addresses.)

Most of the individuals who maintained the attitudes they held as seniors had, in one way or another, created for themselves an environment that reinforced—that is supported and thus continued—the changed attitudes. The study of the husbands was as interesting as anything else. These girls married the "right" kinds of husbands, in that they came from the expected places; more than half of them were from Ivy League colleges. But, to put it a little perversely, they married the wrong kinds of men from the right kinds of colleges (speaking statistically, of course). A comparatively small proportion of them were in any kind of business, and a comparatively large proportion of them were in the professions, especially teaching, in the arts, or in government service. In general it was possible to show that if they did, one way or another, collect the "wrong" kind of husbands—who after all are part of the environment—and found environments that continued to support their changed attitudes, then they didn't change. Not very electrifying, perhaps, but at least it makes sense.

I went to a lot of trouble to find out how, in the 1960 and 1964 elections, people of their social and religious backgrounds—mainly upper-class Protestants, from the Northeast, living in urban and suburban environments—did in fact vote. Here is a quick summary (for which I am indebted to the Survey Research Center of The University of Michigan). In 1960, while the populace at large was voting 50.01 percent for Kennedy, these ex-Bennington people voted 60 percent for Kennedy, whereas people of "their kind" should have voted less than 30 percent. I'm very sure that this is an accurate index. Other people like them—for example, their own sisters and sisters-in-law who didn't go to Bennington—voted less than 30 percent for Kennedy. Their husbands voted 58 percent for Kennedy, and men "like" their husbands in these respects should have voted about 25 percent for Kennedy. In 1964, fewer than 10 percent of these women or their husbands voted for Goldwater.

To the students at Bennington College in the early 1960s, attitudes toward public issues were no longer a concern at all. It could no longer be said, as in the 1930s, that the dominant norms centered around public affairs. I won't say there was noticeable apathy, but there wasn't much *concern*—and for an interesting reason. Most of the students ar-

130

riving at Bennington recently have already become, so to speak, reasonably sophisticated, good little liberals, who come from pleasant, well-read, liberal homes. In August of 1960, before they ever went to college, something like 70 percent of them indicated their preferences for Kennedy, even though a very small percent of them were Catholics.

The norms had changed conspicuously. The contemporary norms were about the kind of an individual one should be. Three notions popped up over and over again in our intensive examination of the problem of contemporary norms. The students emphasized being intellectual, independent, and unconventional. These were norms concerning not public issues but privacy. If I were asked why the norms changed so much in 25 years, I would simply say this: meanwhile, the college had attained a reputation. (I'm sometimes blamed for the kind of reputation that it got, but I refuse to take any particular responsibility for that. After all, I'm only a reporter of what's there!)

At any rate, when the girls first came to Bennington in the 1930s, they came to they knew not what. It had no reputation and only a blurred image. It was totally new. Twenty-five years later it had a reputation and also an image; it was selecting from a quite different set of applicants. For example, there were 3 percent of Jews in the 1930s, 30 percent of Jews in the 1960s. The number of Catholics had also gone up. The percentage of Protestants was down from 85 to about 45. In the 1930s the students, who had a normal, healthy interest in establishing independence, had found that in adopting what was a locally acceptable set of values toward public issues, they could, at the same time, show their independence of their parents—and they did it in droves! But in the early 1960s they couldn't show their independence of their parents in that way. The parents already took liberal positions for granted (perhaps in a slightly smug way)—as if all respectable, thinking, intellectual, independent people were naturally a little left, or a little liberal in one way or another. The students couldn't possibly rebel in that way. But they still had the problem of gaining independence. Becoming independent in an intellectual way and showing one's unconventionality in any personal way one wished to were the things to be striven for.

These patterns emerged because of self-selection on the part of students, and this had enormous effects from the point of view of the things I studied. I knew the admissions policies extremely well when I first went to Bennington. At first they were, inevitably, rather passive ones: we selected in more or less standard ways, somewhat modified by

131

the special characteristics of the college, from those applicants who knew about the college. Essentially, the selection policy hasn't changed much in the 25 years intervening, but the *self*-selection policy has changed a good deal. If this were true all over the country, I should think it would leave admissions officers feeling a little helpless. *If* this was what was happening in Bennington at this particular time, *if* the changes were not the result of planned changes by the admissions office but just happened because of the image, then, insofar as this happens to other places too, the situation does not present a very active, vigorous, prideful picture of what admissions officers do. On the other hand, no admissions officer, I assume, gets away from the problem entirely. The question I want to raise is this: to what extent are admissions officers victims of past images, so that they merely have to pick out "the best" in routine ways of whoever chooses to apply, these choices being made on the basis of past images? I hardly need say, if I may invoke the dinosaur analogy again, that not to develop, not to be planning ways of change, when the world itself is changing at an increasing rate, has its dangers.

Now I turn to another kind of point, having to do with selection of handicapped, ill-prepared students (especially Negroes) in our colleges. It has been pointed out that merely to increase the numbers of such students without any adequate program proposals for a somewhat different selection of students would be folly, indeed. I want to talk about programs to meet needs that exist among certain segments of the population, and about the interdependent problem of programs, needs, and admissions.

By way of illustration, The University of Michigan has just launched what may be called a college within the College of Literature, Science and the Arts. Like any other large university, especially the large state universities, it is increasingly plagued by the impersonality and bureaucracy that come with very large size. Basically, however, it is not sheer size, but the manner of organization that is responsible for its problems. Any university, college, or department can in principle be of any size whatever, provided careful thought has been given to its internal organization.

At any rate, we have, in our own typically Michigan way, spent something like five years planning and designing a program whereby we have what has come to be called a residential college. The official plan is that there will be several of them, each quite distinctive, each having a good deal of autonomy, and each having a reasonably decent

132

human environment within it. A human environment consists of people and what they do, the form and pattern of their interreactions, in college presumably as related to their program.

I'd like to illustrate an example, at my own university, of archaic organization and resulting impersonality and academic anonymity. I made a little calculation as to the probabilities that John Smith and Joe Doakes, who are both in section 78 of English 123, of which there are about 100 sections, will meet each other in any other way on this entire campus—either in other classes or in the same residence. The chances are extremely small. What's the chance that one of them, Joe Doakes, will meet anybody else from section 78 of English 123—anybody else—either in another class or in his residence hall? The chances are a good deal less than 1 in 4 that any freshman in any particular section of a course will ever see any other member of that class, either in another class or in a residence hall, except by chance, on the street. Typically, freshmen in any class never meet except in that class; they are Monday-Wednesday-Friday-at-10 acquaintances. This is what I mean by academic anonymity. Our students, like those in other places, know each other. They have a lively social existence, all kinds of formal and informal pair or group associations that are lively and important to them. The only thing is that these associations have nothing to do with academic life.

There is a movement in this country to what are variously called learning living complexes, cluster arrangements, residential colleges, decentralized academic units, and so forth. It's no accident that the boom, insofar as it is a boom, is appearing in the huge state universities. As a matter of fact, I have, as one of my special projects of late, collated information from all these places that are springing up around the country. And I have a pet bias, which I guess an academic can be forgiven. I have a notion that for the big universities, which are becoming bureaucratic, amorphous, anonymous (and are going to get still more so, if their internal organization is not changed), this movement may be the last gasp of undergraduate education—particularly freshman and sophomore education—within them. That is, if things don't improve, they will turn more toward graduate education. We have a chance, I think, of restoring some of the decency of human environment that still characterizes most of our small colleges. We can recover this kind of decent human environment by judicious use of some devices for reorganization and decentralization.

But this raises an interesting question: how are we going to know

133

whether it works? If this movement is as important as I think it is, these attempts at internal reorganization at various universities need to be assessed. I'm glad to say that plans are already afoot for doing just this. With a bit of luck, we shall have an instance of innovation in higher education that will have been assessed, in a sample of institutions, from the outset.

The college within a college has the advantages not only of restoring a manageable, human environment; of producing a better education, in various ways; and of dealing, somehow, with the leviathan size that is coming to characterize all of the big universities. It has another advantage, which to me almost overshadows all the others. Innovations can take place in a small institution, if plans are started that way. But significant innovation is hard and slow in an established institution. I've known college after college where committees and commissions have spent endless time, conscientiously and ably (even if, perhaps, wrongly), proposing this, that, and the other, with few or no consequences. As one of my colleagues once remarked, after such a failure, "I guess changing our curriculum is something like moving a cemetery."

But suppose that the same proposal were tried in some little unit, off to one side of the university or college. We wouldn't mobilize the same kinds of resistance to it. It could be tried as a little "dry run," and the consequences of its failure would not be regarded as very important. I would assert that if there are to be innovations on the American scene in higher education within the next few years they're going to come mainly in this way. Proud faculties who have interests to maintain and who probably don't quite understand all the purposes of a proposed change are not easy to convince that it ought to be made. But if it has to do with some small part of the institution, if it's frankly proposed as an experiment, and if it isn't going to ruin all these precious ways in which we have learned to live, at least it becomes a possibility.

At any rate, those who are interested in innovations and who do not view with pleasure the prospect of the dinosaur might find this a suitable way to try various kinds of innovations. It won't work for all of them.

I'd like to give an example of one kind of innovation. It has been said that if and when—I think with the emphasis on "if"—American universities had their proper 11 percent of Negro students, we could be encouraged about the state of the disadvantaged. Bearing that in mind, and bearing in mind, also, my deep concern for the possibility of innovative programs, which in turn will effect different kinds of ad-

134

missions policies, I want to offer a proposal. Maybe it's way out, but we won't get anywhere if we don't tolerate way-out ideas. I propose a smallish college unit—called a residential unit, or anything else—that would have the following characteristics. Its admissions policy would be to make it totally representative of that population in American society that has any intentions at all of going to college. I'll say, to be arbitrary, that it would include 11 percent of Negroes. We would deliberately aim at that kind of a cross section. In the second place, since it would have not only Negroes but many other kinds of disadvantaged students, it also would have a plan whereby the older or the more advantaged students, or both, served as tutors or guides and thus gained some practical experience as teachers. Maybe this could be run under the aegis of a department, or a school of education, so that these twin functions could be carried out. Students would be at the same time getting experience as teachers and helping those who needed it.

I see another advantage of a unit like this, which I am speculatively offering. It might be a way of introducing to the community at large a more proper proportion of foreign students. If a proposal like this were educationally satisfactory with a small unit, it would perhaps provide a kind of model to the others. At any rate, it would have provided a supportive environment within the larger one. There has been discussion among admissions officers as to whether it is better for a foreign student to go to a small or large university. It seems to me that an ideal solution would be a small unit within a large university. The small unit, at first, would give the disadvantaged students a supportive environment in which to begin, but with a larger university surrounding it, ambiently, and in which they could eventually move. Moreover, there are advantages not only for the disadvantaged, but also for the advantaged ones.

Whatever kind of college within a college, or unit within a university, that would serve to introduce the kinds of changes that admissions officers need in their own institutions, I suggest that they think of this kind of strategy for doing so.

Perhaps someone is wondering what this proposal has to do with environment. Well, I think of environment simply as the surround—especially as the psychological surround that brings people together. Environment consists not just of people interacting with one another, but we hope of people who are interacting toward the objectives of a program. If I've tried to emphasize anything, it is the interdependence of environment, program, and admissions.

135

If I may quickly draw all my threads together, most colleges are victims of an image that has been previously earned. Sometimes this image is deserved. Nearly always, we're over-proud of it. We overestimate its good qualities. And the consequence is little change. We use such sentences as, "Let's maintain our excellence!"—forgetting about the dinosaurs. I believe too many colleges are trying to be too much alike and are competing for the same students; the consequence is that there are neglected populations of educatees. There are problems that are of importance to society that we are not looking ahead at, and perhaps not even looking behind at, because of the obstacles in the way of innovation.

If we're serious about the neglected populations, about unmet problems, about inadequate planning for change ahead, we shouldn't try to remodel the entire college. We should start with newly organized or reorganized units for which interdependent policies of admission and of program can be simultaneously planned.

Candidate Overlap Studies
and Other Admissions Research

Dean K. Whitla

I would like to organize my remarks around three topics: first, establishing some historical perspective on admissions functions and techniques; second, talking about a current project in which I am intimately involved, which I think addresses itself to the larger problem of research in admissions; and third, looking seriously into some of the areas in which I feel admissions research will make the largest impact in the decade ahead.[1]

Historical Perspective

I have chosen to begin with a historical perspective not primarily because an examination of our heritage can be enlightening in itself but because it helps us to establish a trajectory that may be useful in understanding the directions of research and in contrasting those directions with the needs that we find in society.

I would like to begin by opening the topic beyond the boundaries of admissions research per se and setting it into a total context of ideas and concepts within the behavioral sciences. If I were to think of the ideas that have influenced this world, I am sure I would start with the work of Charles Darwin, whose travels aboard H.M.S. Beagle were a model of superb data collection and whose classic work, *The Origin of Species,* probably has had more impact than any other single volume. While it is a work in biology, it provided a beginning for social science by placing man in a different perspective and allowing him, in a sense forcing him, to become a subject of his own research.

I guess I would follow Darwin with that charming writer, Sigmund Freud, whose work, although preceded by the Greek classics, brought to the attention of the world the importance and complexity of the psychological aspects of human functioning. His spirit of inquiry into

---

1. At this point the participants in the colloquium at Interlochen were asked to complete a two-part questionnaire, the first consisting of some opinions about current practices in American education and the second of questions about the study discussed in this paper. These questionnaire results were tabulated during the period of the address and integrated into the discussion that followed it. The reader might enjoy completing these questions now. If so, the last two pages of the article contain a copy of the questionnaire.

the internal reaches of man's nature has, I think, been a second milestone in establishing the conduct of research in these difficult areas. Whether the basic postulates of Freudian dogma survive does not to my mind lessen the enormous impact of his genius, that the human problem can be attacked with sophistication and that the big questions can be asked. As we think of procedures, techniques, and instruments of admissions, we tend to ignore the fact that we probably rely most heavily in our day-to-day work on a subjective, personal, clinical approach to evaluation and decision making and that Sigmund Freud legitimized that process.

More particularly within our field, we might think back over the history of testing to other periods and other settings. For many centuries, the Chinese governing group was selected through an elaborate series of civil service examinations that were conducted sequentially over a 15-year time period for the candidate. Each successful sitting for an examination was encouraged with a stipend; and so over the period, a young Chinese earned laurels for himself, his family, and his village. Through this procedure of selection and of education, China had the longest living dynasty the world has ever known, and undoubtedly one of the most sophisticated of our cultures, including written language, printing, gunpowder, and a rare lack of nationalism, which ultimately led to the downfall of the four-thousand-year-old dynasty when it was unable to cope with the English opium war.

In the modern Western tradition, I would probably start with the work of Sir Francis Galton, a cousin of Darwin. Galton began examining individual differences in man, measuring the size of skull, strength of grip, tapping speed, use of symbols, reaction time, vision, hearing, and ability to use words, read diagrams, and solve problems. In France several years later, Alfred Binet became a member of a commission to determine which children were able to profit from regular school instruction, and which were not; to do so he established a series of tests. For example, from the age of 3 to 6, he found that children should be able to state the family name, identify familiar objects, copy figures, and obey commands. At the age of 10–11, they should be able to name the months in order, recognize coins, and make up sentences with key words. Interestingly, he used the concept of the work sample to construct his tests because it is impossible to measure intelligence directly. Just as a cloud chamber does not permit a physicist to see the atom but rather it is the ionizing particles that reveal tracks so that he can deduce the nature of the atom, so must we examine the

138

nature of intelligence by its manifestation in specific behaviors. Edward Thorndike probably developed most clearly the measurement of intelligence and specifically, quantitative evaluation. He felt that there were three types of intelligence: abstract or verbal, practical, and social. Charles Spearman sought to show through his work that intellectual abilities are a function of two factors, one general (g) factor common to every ability and specific (s) factors particular to every ability. David Wechsler claims that (g) is one of the great discoveries of psychology. Since that time there has been much controversy over the nature of intelligence ranging from Wechsler's concept of global intelligence to J. P. Guilford's multifactored domain.

Particularly within the admissions area, there was the work of Carl Brigham, who thought aptitude test results for scholarship applicants to Princeton University might be useful to the admissions committee. They did find such results helpful, and out of this beginning was born the College Board Scholastic Aptitude Test. For years the SAT included a morning session of multiple-choice aptitude tests and an afternoon session of subject-matter essay tests. On the day of Pearl Harbor, a committee was deliberating about whether the College Board Achievement Tests ought to be placed in the multiple-choice form, for it was very difficult to find sufficient numbers of readers to handle the essay form. Because of that fateful day, the decision was made to put the Achievement Tests into a multiple-choice format. At the same time, the standard for the SAT scale was established, and students taking the test in 1941 made up the base group on which the mean was established as 500 with the standard deviation of 100. While the fixed scale has been a very necessary property of the test, it has had some unfortunate connotations for the unwary; for a score of 500 is only the average of that basic norm group. If all seniors in high school were to take the test, the mean would be approximately 375 with a standard deviation of 120, which is vastly different from the usual norms that we think of for the test. Similarly, a mean of 375 is much higher than is the mean for the total age group.

It was necessary to establish a constant scale for the SAT so that a candidate would not be handicapped because of the norming of a particular test administration where the test might be standardized on a group of very bright fellow students or a relatively poor group. If the norming varied, it would be impossible for admissions officers to make any evaluation of scores from test to test and from year to year. There has now been developed a very elaborate system of keeping the scale

139

constant, called "double part score equating," which is really a system of using some items from previous tests—some from the father and grandfather tests—and even more complicated lineages that minimize the drift in score change. This practice, plus elaborate security measures, make the SAT a very expensive test. It seems to me worth the cost, for it minimizes the games that can be played in admissions, an area that is full of social cost and already fraught with many games and gamesmen.

I would like to cite some of the basic procedures that I think have been responses to research findings as well as responsiveness of organizations to the needs of admissions. On this list I would put such things as the College Board College Scholarship Service, Advanced Placement Examinations, *Manual of Freshman Class Profiles*, and Validity Study Service; the College Admissions Center of the Association of College Admission Counselors; and national scholarship programs. I think the impact of these on admissions practices has been to move us from localism to a national viewpoint, to move admissions itself from a privileged process to one of meritocracy, and to move colleges from isolated activities to cooperative ventures. I think that as we have changed the criteria of our decisions, we have helped to improve the quality of both secondary and college education.

Study of Candidate Overlap

In recent years several trends have combined to place considerable strain on the annual process whereby more than a million youth move from school to college. The proportion of the age group entering higher education has increased steadily; higher institutions have increased in number, size, and diversity; increasing mobility of students has highlighted the variety of procedures used by different colleges, and there has been increasing social pressure on students to gain admission to one of the limited number of well-known institutions. In response to the commonly perceived "admissions problem," there has been a variety of cooperative efforts to streamline admissions procedures. Many of these efforts have failed because of the complexities of the problem and the difficulty in finding solutions that are acceptable to a number of institutions.

The admissions problem is now becoming accepted as not one problem but a variety of problems requiring different solutions for different groups of institutions. While this approach is certainly more reasonable than applying single solutions to all colleges, it does illustrate the

140

need for more objective information concerning the similarities among institutions with respect to their characteristics, objectives, and particularly the populations of students they serve.

Except in isolated cases admissions officers have been forced to guess at the extent of overlap between their admitted students and those of other institutions. Without such information it has been quite difficult to determine whether or not common application forms, admissions centers, or cooperative arrangements would actually benefit a given group of colleges and their applicants. Colleges have also been reluctant to make worthwhile changes in their admissions procedures or requirements because of uncertainty regarding the effects such changes might have on an unknown group of applicants presumably shared with competing institutions.

In 1965 at an Ivy League meeting it was proposed that we make a study of our mutual applicants. The eight colleges plus M.I.T. agreed to prepare cards according to a specified format and forward them to Cambridge for processing. While there were innumerable problems in procedure (everyone used a different system for coding rank in class; we spelled names differently, sometimes using initials, sometimes names, which made it very difficult for the computer) the results were of sufficient interest to invite continuation. To solve our procedural problems we decided it would be wise to request a second set of score cards, to be generated by Educational Testing Service so that formats would be identical.

Our discussion went by way of the College Board where the idea of expanding the study into a larger pilot project was well received, and the Board became an active supporter and financial participant. Without attempting to justify the specific colleges invited to participate, we began by soliciting the cooperation of the Eastern Group of Admissions Directors (EGADs!)[2] and extended this list south and west to colleges with which we anticipated we would have common candidates. We ended up with a list of 43, and formulated a plan of action for collecting, analyzing, and reporting comprehensive information regarding the nature and extent of candidate overlap among this group of colleges and universities. As an ultimate purpose we saw the development of an information system that would:

1. Permit any admissions officer to examine his applicant group periodically in reference to each other institution with respect to com-

---

2. Hobart College was omitted inadvertently and we apologize for this.

mon applicants, admissions decisions, students' decisions, and the characteristics of students falling into the various overlapping categories.

2. Produce a variety of empirical groupings of institutions on the basis of different types of overlap or the characteristics of the students who constitute the overlap.

The numerous and intricate problems of style, timing, procedures, and purposes that characterize the admissions process certainly would not be solved merely by the compilations of relevant information. There was reason to hope, however, that admissions officers would be better able to judge the effects of their procedures and the possible value of cooperative agreements if appropriate descriptions of overlapping candidates among institutions were available.

Participating colleges. The following 43 colleges participated in this study:

Alfred	Carnegie	Grinnell	Princeton	Tufts
Amherst	Chicago	Hamilton	Reed	Union
Antioch	Clarkson	Harvard	R.P.I. (N.Y.)	U. of Cal.
Bates	Colby	Haverford	Rice	(Berkeley)
Bowdoin	Colgate	Lafayette	Rochester	U. of Penn.
Brown	Columbia	Lehigh	Stanford	Wesleyan
Bucknell	Cornell	M.I.T.	Swarthmore	Williams
Cal. Tech.	Dartmouth	Oberlin	Syracuse	Yale
Carleton	Duke	Pomona	Trinity (Conn.)	

Procedure. The punched score cards from all administrations of the SAT during the academic year 1965-66 were the basic data input for the analysis. Each of the colleges received score reports for its applicants and was asked to separate them into four groups according to admission status:

1. students accepting offers of admission,
2. students admitted but going elsewhere,
3. rejected applicants,
4. those who did not complete an application.

In total, about 268,000 score reports were received from the 43 participating colleges.

The first step in the analysis was the reducing of the score reports to yield a single record for each candidate. This was achieved by a computer sort on name and birth date followed by a matching operation on the same variables plus a candidate's social security and secondary school code numbers. The lowest acceptable criterion for a

142

"match" condition was the same name and secondary school code. However, it was necessary to accept this least reliable match in only about 1 percent of the cases. In 75 percent of the "matches" the full complement of information was identical. Most of the remaining "matches" were made in the absence only of the social security number. The data reduction phase resulted in a shrinkage to 165,000 unique individuals from the 268,000 score reports. Of the 165,000 individuals who forwarded scores to the colleges, there were 78,000 who completed their application and on whom admissions decisions were made. I shall limit this discussion to these 78,000 individuals who filed applications for admission as freshmen for the year of 1966-67.

Overview. We began with an overview of the 78,000 applicants on whom the colleges made admissions decisions. These 78,000 applicants filed 129,000 applications or made an average of 1.65 applications per person. In studies for candidates to Ivy League colleges we found the average number of applications filed there to be similar. The figures for Ivy colleges were 1.55 in 1965 as compared with this number of 1.65 a year later. This was undoubtedly less than the total number of applications that were made by the candidates, for many would have made applications in addition to those filed to this group of 43 colleges. It is interesting to note that data compiled on the frequency of multiple applications always seem to reveal smaller numbers than those of us engaged in the process expect. The Project Talent data tend to confirm this; it was found that only slightly over one application was made by students around the country who were planning to attend college. The financial information recorded by the College Scholarship Service indicates that there is an average of 1.9 applications per candidate.

Table 1. Multiple Applications

	Applications filed										
	1	2	3	4	5	6	7	8	9	10	11
Candidates	48,881	16,450	7,709	3,547	1,265	425	134	33	6	4	2
Percent of all candidates	62.3	21.0	9.8	4.5	1.6	0.5	0.2	0.0	0.0	0.0	0.0

Table 1 shows that 48,881, or 62 percent, of this group of candidates filed only 1 application, while there were two students who filed 11 applications to the 43 colleges. On the one hand, the number of mul-

143

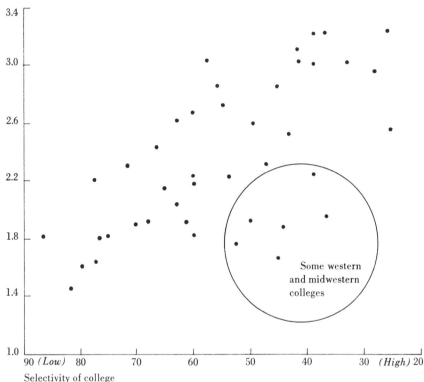

Figure 1. College Selectivity and Multiple Applications

Average
number of
applications
filed to all
colleges by
candidates
to a specific
college

Some western
and midwestern
colleges

Selectivity of college

● represents a college

tiple applications does not seem excessive, considering the fact that 93 percent of the group filed 3 or fewer applications. On the other hand, one can view with some alarm the fact that as many as 2.3 percent did make 5 or more applications to these 43 colleges.

Another noteworthy piece of information is the fact that candidates who apply to certain colleges make more applications than do those

144

applying to others of this group. For example, on the average, students applying to Amherst, Bowdoin, Haverford, Williams, or Yale make more than 3 applications.

To examine the apparent phenomenon that applicants to competitive colleges file more applications than do students to colleges in general, we built a selectivity index composed of three parts: (1) percent of total admitted, (2) percent of applicants with scores less than 600, and (3) percent of applicants scoring over 700 and rejected.

We plotted (see Figure 1) this index against the average number of applications filed per candidate. The relationship is pronounced; if one is interested in a highly selective college, one takes care to file his credentials in numerous places. The relationship would be more pronounced if geographical location of the colleges did not appear to play a role; some midwestern and western colleges have been circled to show that much of the traffic flow around them was not included.

We also examined the application patterns according to the type of school attended (independent or public) and SAT scores. Those who attended independent schools made on the average 1.95 applications, while those from public schools made 1.62. And correspondingly the percentage of students filing 3 or more applications was larger from the independent school population than from the public schools. We divided the candidates according to their SAT verbal scores and found that the higher the score, the larger the number of applications. Those with scores under 600 filed on the average 1.5 applications, those with scores between 600 and 700 filed 1.8 applications, and those with scores over 700 filed over 2 applications on the average.

Table 2. Multiple Applications by Scores and Schooling

SAT-*verbal scores*	Applications per candidate	
	Public school	Private school
700 or higher	2.00	2.29
600-699	1.78	2.13
Lower than 600	1.49	1.81
Average	1.62	1.95

We examined the interrelationship between school affiliation and scores and found that the trend was consistent: the increase in applications was equally pronounced at various score intervals for both public and private students. These findings tend to refute some of the more common mythology about the multiple application syndrome, that it is the student who can ill afford psychologically or financially to make multiple applications who actually does make many college applications. These data, while unfortunately limited in scope, say just the opposite, that it is the more talented student (using a simple index of College Board test scores), coming from a more privileged background (as indexed by attendance at an independent school) who tends to make the larger number of applications. It could be argued that these findings are simply an artifact of the grouping and that since these are mainly private colleges, this is where private students apply. Since these institutions tend to be selective, students with poorer scores merely make a try while filing their serious applications elsewhere. We think it would be an oversimplification to say that students scoring 400-500 tend to file a wild card application with this group of colleges in their search for an admission ticket. They file on the average 1.5 applications, which is considerably above a wild card base line; 12 percent, as a matter of fact, file 3 or more applications. In addition, in today's world it is the able student who is actively sought. For example, a National Merit Scholarship semifinalist may receive, because of his award, recruiting letters from 30 colleges. The students aware of their desirability may tend to apply to several colleges, more so than their less able fellows.

Table 3. Multiple Admissions

Applicants offered admission—41,929
Number of admissions offers—55,828

	Number of admissions							
	0	1	2	3	4	5	6	7
Number of candidates	36,527	31,772	7,247	2,243	539	97	25	6
Percent of all candidates	46.6	40.5	9.2	2.9	0.7	0.1	0.0	0.0

Using the same kind of procedure, we examined the number of admissions offers made to these candidates. Of the 78,000 applicants, 42,000 were offered admission, and they received 56,000 admissions offers. Fifty-three percent were offered admission to at least one of these 43 colleges, and 47 percent were rejected.[3] Forty-one percent of

---

3. I think that on first blush everybody is bothered by the fact that 47 percent of these applicants are not offered admission to any one of these colleges. While that is an understandable reaction, clearly such an interpretation does not acknowledge the microcosmic nature of this group of 43 and correspondingly not the admissions action beyond this group.

146

this total group received one admissions offer, 9 percent two offers, 3 percent three offers, and less than 1 percent four or more. There were six candidates who were offered admission to seven of these colleges. We find, then, a very small number receiving several admissions offers. There seems to be a surprisingly large dispersion of available spaces among the candidate group. The social waste so often mentioned does not occur at this stage, for these colleges have in fact offered admission to more students than they can enroll; shrinkage as a result of candidacy overlap has been included in their planning. At this point in the admissions process we only have fortunate students who have an opportunity to choose among several offers.

Table 4. Multiple Admissions by Scores and Schooling

| | Percent of candidates admitted | |
SAT-*verbal scores*	*Public school*	*Private school*
700 or higher	79	82
600-699	66	67
Lower than 600	45	41

Table 4 shows some very remarkable findings. Of those candidates who attended public schools and whose SAT-verbal scores were in the 400-500s, 45 percent were offered admission. Of those whose scores were between 600 and 700, 66 percent were offered admission; of those with scores over 700, 79 percent were offered admission. A very similar pattern exists for those who attended private schools: of those with scores under 600, 41 percent were offered admission; of those with scores between 600-700, 67 percent were offered admission; and of those with scores over 700, 82 percent were offered admission. This documents impressively the similarity between the admissions rates for public and independent school candidates. The differences in rates favored, in the bottom category, those from the public schools by a margin of 4 percent. In the middle score category private school applicants were favored by 1 percent, and in the top score bracket, they were favored by 3 percent. In other words, for this group of 78,000 applicants the differences in admissions rates of those who attended public and private schools are nil; according to score level the differences are very pronounced.[4]

While no set of statistics can ever answer the complicated question that many parents ask about where their children should be educated,

---

4. A study of Ivy League college data produced the same finding.

this does approach one facet of the problem. Clearly it is the quality of performance rather than the type of school attended that is significant in the admissions process. It is impossible from these data to explore the more complicated business of whether the same boy would have received a 700 score had he gone to a public school rather than to an independent school or vice versa. These results focus only on the reaction of the admissions committees when viewing candidates and, in spite of this superficial manner of categorizing candidates, do show the equality in admissions standards.

Before going on to a factor analysis of these data, I would like to summarize the responses of the admissions officers at Interlochen (see footnote 1) to the questions covering the information I have just presented.

1. How many applications did the average candidate to these colleges file to this group of 43?
   (1) 1, (2) 1, (3) 15, (4) 18, (5) 11, (6) 3, (7) 1.
   The answer was 1.65.

2. What percentage of these candidates filed more than three applications to these colleges?
   (0-10%) 6, (11-20%) 5, (21-30%) 3, (31-40%) 3, (41-50%) 4, (51-60%) 10, (61-70%) 6, (71-80%) 8, (81-90%) 4, (91-100%) 2.
   The answer was 6.8%.

3. What is the relationship between the selectivity of a college to which an applicant applies and the number of applications he makes?
   Selectivity has little relationship to number of applications filed—16.
   If selectivity is high, the number of applications is large—27 (correct choice).
   If selectivity is low, the number of applications is large—5.

4. Public school candidates make more _____ fewer _____ applications than private school candidates.
   More—17
   Fewer—31 (correct choice)
   Same—1

5. Those candidates with high scores make more _____ fewer _____ applications than those with low scores.
   More—29 (correct choice)
   Fewer—21

148

6. What percentage of candidates receive three or more admissions tickets?

(1-5%) 3, (6-10%) 5, (11-20%) 10, (21-30%) 2, (31-40%) 10, (41-50%) 15, (51-60%) 2, (70-80%) 3.

The correct answer was 3.7%.

7. How much more important for admissions is it to have a 700+ score than a 500-600 SAT-V score?

Increases the odds 5 times—14

Increases the odds 3 times—10

Increases the odds 2 times—22 (correct choice)

Increases the odds negligibly—4

8. How much more important for admissions is it to have attended private school than public school?

Three times as important—0

Twice as important—20

Is of no advantage—26 (correct choice)

Is a handicap—4

Looking at this recapitulation of study results and participant responses, I notice that the surprising findings of this study pertain to the small number of students filing multiple applications and in turn how seldom students are offered admission to a number of colleges. The guesses of this sophisticated group of admissions officers[5] do leave one with the feeling that we need extensive exploration of the parameters of the admissions scene. If experts in the field harbor misconceptions, it is small wonder that the populace as a whole has a distorted view of the American college-going process.

Factor analysis. There are many ways of representing associations among colleges: by major purposes, by geographical location, by size, by athletic associations. The series of associations drawn from the pattern of applications provides another and provocative representation. Normally one thinks of students applying to colleges of varying competitiveness in admissions rather than to equally competitive institutions. The data I am about to present tell a different story. The groupings, as I will demonstrate, seem horizontal (that is, students apply to colleges that are equally competitive in admissions) and logical, and

---

5. While I have never before formally asked knowledgeable persons to answer such questions, I have found the same degree of discrepancy occurring on informal occasions with a wide range of admissions personnel.

149

provide another source of evidence to strengthen the existing regional and stylistic associations.

We selected factor analysis as a method of formalizing our observations about the dyadic patterns of applications; and it was with care that we attempted to select a measure that would accurately represent the relationship of overlapping candidacy without being biased by the differences simply in the size of the college candidate body. We eliminated from consideration the candidates who made only one application, for unique candidates would tell us nothing about overlap.

Factor analysis was chosen as an analytic technique because it is an effective mathematical method for summarizing complex quantitative data. It summarizes by extracting information common to a series of variables. On a dimension, or technically on an axis, certain variables emerge as "heavily loaded" or "weighted." Thus, in this case we see which colleges are heavily weighted and in this sense cluster together because of the presence of mutual applicants.

Comments on pattern analysis—total applicants.[6] From the first solution we obtained six factors. As traditional with factor solutions, it is difficult to establish cutting lines so we have used three criteria: first, those colleges with high loadings, which are most strongly associated with the factor; second, relatively high association (usually the highest loading obtained for the college); third, a linkage group—colleges with higher loadings elsewhere but significant loadings on this factor.

The first factor is essentially an Ivy League group (in addition to Ivy schools, Amherst, Wesleyan, and Williams appear). The colleges with relatively high association on this factor are Haverford, Trinity, Tufts, Colgate, and Hamilton; those that form linkage between two factors are Cornell and Penn, which are also very strongly associated with Factor V, and Bowdoin, which also loads heavily on Factor VI. Factor II consists of a West Coast grouping. Factor III emphasizes a cluster of science-oriented colleges. Factor IV tends to be small midwestern selective colleges. Factor V is formed of Pennsylvania and New York state schools and Factor VI, the Down East triumvirate Bates, Bowdoin, and Colby linked to Tufts.

Comments on phi analysis — all applicants.[7] We now have essentially

---

6. Analysis based on correlations between numbers of applicants common to pairs of colleges.

7. Analysis based on phi coefficients between numbers of applicants common to a pair of colleges.

Pattern Analysis—All Applicants

	Factor I	Factor II	Factor III	Factor IV	Factor V	Factor VI
Most strongly associated	Yale, Harvard, Princeton, Amherst, Dartmouth, Williams, Brown, Wesleyan, Columbia	Stanford, U. of Cal. (Berkeley), Pomona, Reed	M.I.T., R.P.I. (N.Y.), Cal. Tech., Carnegie	Oberlin, Swarthmore, Antioch, Chicago, Grinnell, Carleton	Cornell, Syracuse, U. of Penn., Rochester, Bucknell	Colby, Bates, Bowdoin
Relatively high association	Haverford, Trinity (Conn.), Tufts, Colgate, Hamilton	Cal. Tech., Rice	Clarkson, Rice		Lehigh, Lafayette, Alfred, Duke	
Linkage	Bowdoin, U. of Penn., Cornell		Cornell	Columbia, Reed, Harvard	Tufts, Columbia	Tufts

151

Phi Analysis—All Applicants

	Factor I	Factor II	Factor III	Factor IV	Factor V	Factor VI	Factor VII
Most strongly associated	Williams	Stanford	M.I.T.	Oberlin	Colby	Bucknell	Harvard
	Wesleyan	Pomona	R.P.I. (N.Y.)	Carleton	Bates	Syracuse	Yale
	Amherst	U. of Cal. (Berkeley)	Carnegie	Grinnell	Bowdoin	Lehigh	Princeton
	Trinity (Conn.)		Clarkson	Swarthmore		Lafayette	Columbia
	Hamilton		Cal. Tech.	Antioch		Cornell	Brown
	Colgate			Chicago		U. of Penn.	
	Dartmouth					Rochester	
Relatively high association	Union		Rice	Reed	Tufts	Duke	
				Haverford		Alfred	
Linkage	Bowdoin	Cal. Tech.				Colgate	U. of Penn.
	Lafayette	Reed					Cornell
	Brown						Dartmouth
							Amherst
							Chicago

152

two Ivy groups—Factors I and VII. Factor II is still the West Coast and Factor III, the schools with a scientific orientation. Factor IV is the original midwest–liberal–selective college group, Factor V, the Down East triumvirate, and Factor VI, the New York–Pennsylvania state cluster.

We made several other factor solutions; however, the results were so clearly overlapping with those already presented that they are currently omitted. The factors were quite consistent; a prominent and ever-present factor was that of the Ivy group; occasionally it seemed to break into two factors. Depending on the style of analysis, the magnitude of the loading reshuffled the order of the colleges. A West Coast factor appeared in every analysis. California Institute of Technology sometimes shifted from this factor to the persistent third factor—the scientifically oriented schools.

The fourth association was among a group of colleges of wide geographical spread; these tended to be small–liberal–selective. The membership in this group was sensitive to the style of analysis and shifted more than that in any of the other factors.

One surprising development was the split at times of the New York–Pennsylvania factor. Occasionally these colleges grouped together. At other times, they separated. And at times only the Pennsylvania grouping was strong enough to produce a factor. We have always known that the Down East triumvirate of Colby, Bates, and Bowdoin existed; to find that the factor solution produced this verity lends a sense of validity to the total process.

To illustrate some of the complexities underlying the simply demonstrated patterns, I've included a plot of Factors I and IV (Figure 2). It shows that while Yale and Harvard are heavily loaded on Factor I, they also load on the second factor, especially Harvard. Columbia and Haverford tend to bridge between Factors I and IV. Antioch has a negative loading on the first factor. Yale, Harvard, and Princeton applications imply that candidates to these schools will not also apply as frequently to Antioch or vice versa. Colleges with a negative loading on Factor IV are Trinity, Bowdoin, Colgate, Hamilton, implying that Oberlin–Swarthmore–Chicago–Antioch applicants would not apply as frequently to these other four colleges and vice versa.

The phi analysis comparison of Factors I and V illustrates much the same complexity (Figure 3); it shows that Bates and Colby are quite separate from Bowdoin, which loads substantially in the Factor I space. Bowdoin, Tufts, and Brown tend to bridge between Factors I and V.

153

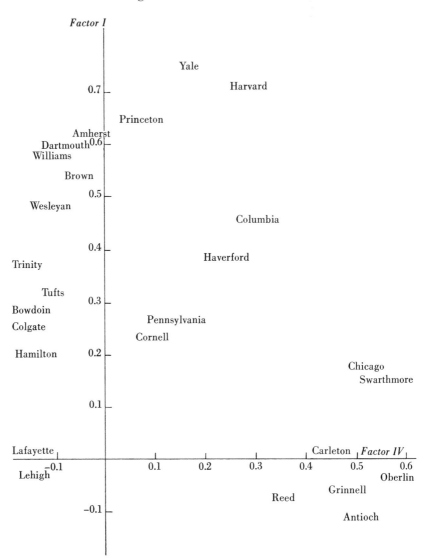

Figure 2. Pattern Analysis — All Applicants
Rotated Factor Loadings — Factor I vs. IV

154

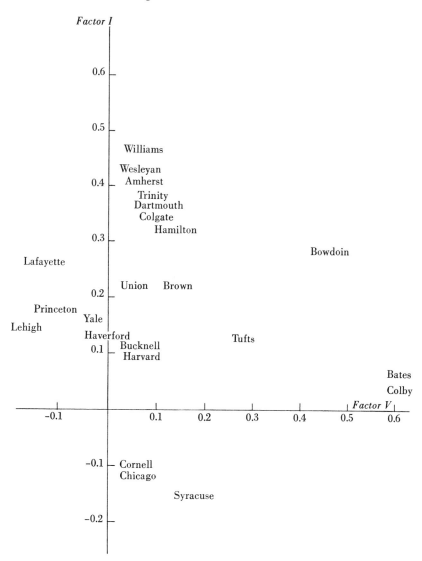

Figure 3. Phi Analysis — All Applicants
Rotated Factor Loadings — Factor I vs. V

We also can see here the negative loading of certain schools: Lafayette–Princeton–Lehigh load negatively on the Bates–Colby factor. The same is true of Factor I, where Cornell–Chicago–Syracuse load negatively.

I have not discussed the utility of these findings to admissions people in terms of their own colleges. What the findings reveal is the tendency toward a horizontal application pattern; there is little evidence of students cross filing to colleges of differing styles. The colloquial phrase "shooting one application 'up,' one on the 'level,' and one 'down,'" does not seem to apply; rather, when a student is attracted to a particular style of college he tends to apply to several of that group. Second, this study contains some hard data for thinking about the magnitude of overlap, where it exists, and the real cause and source of admissions confusion. The estimates made by admissions officers lead me to believe that such knowledge can help to clarify misconceptions about college admissions. Third, the findings provide another rationale for establishing cooperative ventures in colleges: the data suggest that such ventures should in part transcend geographical location, and that such a basis would be a sensible one for college cooperation. This way of looking at a college's style reflects an applicant's perception of a school. He's investing an application fee, he's taking a day or two to make out application forms, he is telling the College Board that he wants scores sent to that college, and he is taking something of a psychic gamble in making an application. Clearly he has given time and energy and probably some real thought to the application, and consequently admissions officers cannot dismiss lightly the perceptions that he has about the college.

Research in the Decade Ahead

I will use the six questions on Part I of the questionnaire, and the responses of admissions officers at Interlochen (see footnote 1), as a springboard for talking about research in the decade ahead.

1. Undergraduate colleges will disappear as anything other than pre-professional education.

    Agree—1
    Tend to agree—7
    Neutral—2
    Tend to disagree—16
    Disagree—26

156

If this were to come about, do you feel that for American education it would be:

Advantageous—1
Tend to be advantageous—6
Neutral—1
Tend to be disadvantageous—18
Disadvantageous—24

The responses of the colloquium participants indicate that they clearly feel that undergraduate education has an identity in its own right and will not disappear during the next decade. The predictions by Jacques Barzun are unlikely to be fulfilled, according to this group, and would be disadvantageous if they were to take place. My personal feeling is that there will be a resurgence of emphasis on the undergraduate years in the next decade much as there has been on the secondary school years in this last decade. I think that there will also be considerable research evidence accumulated during this period to show the importance of those particular years.

The work of Erik H. Erikson[8] currently shows the importance of the moratorium during this period when the student is extracted from the family, develops his own set of values, and goes through the process of making decisions about vocation, life, and raison d'être before fully accepting the responsibilities of a job and family. This phenomenon seems to be present in almost every culture in some form, and as our own culture becomes more complex I think that it is necessary to institutionalize this process. The college years seem to be a very appropriate time for the moratorium in terms of the stage of psychological development and in view of the college itself as an institution. I think that additional research currently being conducted in this area will lend greater credence to Erikson's hypothesis.

Second, I think that in the very new area of cognitive development, evidence will indicate that there is a certain mastery of material that can take place most effectively during these years. While this new understanding of cognitive style might be used profitably in the pursuit of preprofessional knowledge, I think that it will be found to be more effectively used if the scope is broader and more typical of that that we normally term liberal education.

---

8. "Identity and the Life Cycle, Selected Papers," *Psychological Issues*, Vol. 1, No. 1, Monograph 1, 1959, pp. 18-173.

2. The private sector of education will continue to decrease.
     Agree—19
     Tend to agree—22
     Neutral—2
     Tend to disagree—3
     Disagree—5

   If this were to come about, do you feel that for American education it would be:
     Advantageous—0
     Tend to be advantageous—1
     Neutral—2
     Tend to be disadvantageous—17
     Disadvantageous—29

   The participants felt that the question would have been easier to answer if it had been phrased more specifically; in terms of numbers of students or percentage of students; in terms of higher education or four-year colleges. Undoubtedly these ambiguities have produced the varieties in answers seen above. The more interesting answers are to the second portion of the question; essentially, the participants thought reduction in private education would be an unfortunate occurrence on the American educational scene.

   The recent and continuing establishment of new private colleges in this time of inflated educational costs does seem a bit surprising. But much more surprising is the presence of new private secondary schools in the deprived areas of center cities. These areas have long been conceded to be the heart of the public sector, and private education has been considered the anathema of their populaces. Clearly the new schools are being responsive to local needs and may well disappear as quickly as they were created when public education does become responsive.

   The concept of competition now being advocated by Edgar Friedenberg and Theodore Sizer brings a new view to education. They propose that monies be freed from the public sector so that private education may become a viable alternative to public education.

3. Programed instruction, computer-aided instruction, and prepackaged courses will become the grand equalizers; hence, the opportunity for intellectual encounters will be the same in all colleges.
     Agree—1

158

Tend to agree—6
Neutral—0
Tend to disagree—19
Disagree—24

If this were to come about, do you feel that for American education it would be:

Advantageous—0
Tend to be advantageous—6
Neutral—3
Tend to be disadvantageous—14
Disadvantageous—25

The preponderance of participants said that the grand equalizers would not make all colleges the same and that if they were to do so, it would be disadvantageous. Questions were raised about whether the second part of the statement necessarily followed from the first. It was intended that the second part would be essentially explanatory of the concept of the grand equalizer, for by these new methods of instruction it might be possible for all students—regardless of college attended—to have the same intellectual opportunity. This is the big research question of the decade, one on which industry is prepared to spend at least a billion dollars, and it behooves all of us to keep as well informed about it as possible.

4. A national admissions system such as the UCCA (University College Center for Admissions) in England will be functioning within the next decade or so.

Agree—3
Tend to agree—8
Neutral—13
Tend to disagree—10
Disagree—13

If this were to come about, do you feel that for American education it would be:

Advantageous—3
Tend to be advantageous—13
Neutral—7
Tend to be disadvantageous—10
Disadvantageous—15

My feeling is that we should have such a system as soon as it is needed

159

and not a moment before. The study I described is, I think, a useful device in giving us information about the need for such a system. From that evidence, the conclusion I draw is that a national system is not needed and that local cooperative ventures would be much more appropriate responses to current needs.

5. The impact of Head Start and other programs for the disadvantaged will provide such opportunities that this group will be able to take their rightful place in the educational stream by the time of their college years.

    Agree—4
    Tend to agree—16
    Neutral—3
    Tend to disagree—18
    Disagree—4

I wish I could be as optimistic as a number of the participants. Personally, I would say that there was not a chance. The recent work at ETS on the bias in the SAT has shown that there are no particular sets of items that are particularly difficult for the disadvantaged; second, tutoring experiments have shown that it is not the unusual form of the test that seems to be especially difficult for the disadvantaged; third, a look at John Hills' data[9] on the university system in Georgia shows that scores are predictive of academic performance for the disadvantaged, as they are for any other group. These all add up to a dismal outlook. Even new analysis being made of the Higher Horizons data raises a lot of questions about the original enthusiastic interpretation of those programs. Our hope these days seems to be tied to some of the newer programs under way: the work of Martin Deutsch and Carl Bereiter.[10] In these programs as well as programs in several colleges around the country, there are hopeful exceptions to the generally dismal record. At the moment it is difficult to generalize, especially from these latter exceptions. Clearly, the unfortunate, cyclic pattern of development of the disadvantaged is one of the nation's biggest internal problems and one that research must help us to solve. Each of us is trying in his own way to make some progress on this

---

9. J. R. Hills, J. A. Kloch, and M. L. Bush, *Counselor's Guide to Georgia Colleges.* Atlanta: Office of Testing and Guidance, University System of Georgia, 1965, p. 60.
10. Carl Bereiter and S. Engleman, *Teaching Disadvantaged Children in Preschool.* Englewood Cliffs: Prentice-Hall, Inc., 1966, 312 pp. Martin Deutsch, *Disadvantaged Child.* New York: Basic Books, Inc., 1967, 400 pp.

160

problem. I am sure that we will soon have processes for making better evaluations of the effect of the press of college on people from disadvantaged backgrounds so that we can have information useful to the decision process. We will have some new ideas about how the whole educational process must change to reflect the needs of the disadvantaged. And maybe we shall have to conclude with Bruno Bettleheim that the Head Start program comes too late in a child's life.

6. During the decade ahead we will have available innumerable methods for judging the qualities of college environments and the personal styles of applicants; this should markedly increase the effectiveness of the admissions process.

    Agree—11
    Tend to agree—25
    Neutral—2
    Tend to disagree—11
    Disagree—2

If this were to come about, do you feel that for American education it would be:

    Advantageous—18
    Tend to be advantageous—22
    Neutral—4
    Tend to be disadvantageous—3
    Disadvantageous—1

I am not as optimistic about the favorable outcomes as this group of participants. Of course, there will be many more instruments for judging environments and applicants. Such instruments as CUES (College and University Environment Scales) and OAIS (Opinion, Attitude and Interest Survey) are now available for the examination of both the college press and the students' values. But for all this work, results from these instruments still seem to leave more variance unexplained than one would anticipate, and we have little idea of how to use their findings at the moment.

We in Cambridge have given some thought to the process of constructing the class — as has everyone — and we think we have become a little more sophisticated than just using variables, such as economic diversity, geographic distribution, and college major. We like to think that a useful concept is the psychological impact on a student of his academic standing in his class. Fred Glimp, formerly dean of admissions at Harvard,[11] has called this "the search for the happy bottom quarter type." We have found that there are students who because of their previous performance come expecting to rank very well in their class. When they find that there are many students above them, they tend to feel second rate. This psychological impact of averageness becomes even more pronounced near the bottom, especially when students are interested in going on to graduate school and there seems to be an inadequate supply of psychic rewards. In an attempt to discover some solution, we have struck upon the idea of admitting students whose talents do not lie especially in the area of academic work, but whose great strength in other areas more than compensates, making them attractive individuals personally and effective in their own area. We hope that such students will not be disturbed by their rank in class, but will go through their four undergraduate years enjoying the experience and getting a great deal out of it, later making a marked contribution to the world because of the experience despite the fact that they do not graduate with honors. In contrast, the men whom we might have taken in their places have gone elsewhere where they can achieve many of the distinctions that are rightfully theirs.

The very tenor of my remarks must indicate that I am optimistic about the future contributions of research to these several areas. The factors that will lead to successful resolution of our problems will be the continual interaction between research and practice. Only through an interchange essentially symbiotic in nature will we effectively attack the major problems in American education.

---

11. Currently dean of Harvard College.

162

Part I. The first set of six questions was written to get your opinions on some current truisms in American education.

1. Undergraduate colleges will disappear as anything other than prepro-fessional education.

    Agree—; Tend to agree—; Neutral—; Tend to disagree—;
    Disagree—

    If this were to come about, do you feel that for American education it would be:

    Advantageous—; Tend to be advantageous—; Neutral—;
    Tend to be disadvantageous—; Disadvantageous—

2. The private sector of education will continue to decrease.

    Agree—; Tend to agree—; Neutral—; Tend to disagree—;
    Disagree—

    If this were to come about, do you feel that for American education it would be:

    Advantageous—; Tend to be advantageous—; Neutral—;
    Tend to be disadvantageous—; Disadvantageous—

3. Programed instruction, computer-aided instruction, and prepackaged courses will become the grand equalizers; hence, the opportunity for intellectual encounters will be the same in all colleges.

    Agree—; Tend to agree—; Neutral—; Tend to disagree—;
    Disagree—

    If this were to come about, do you feel that for American education it would be:

    Advantageous—; Tend to be advantageous—; Neutral—;
    Tend to be disadvantageous—; Disadvantageous—

4. A national admissions system such as the UCCA (University College Center for Admissions) in England will be functioning within the next decade or so.

    Agree—; Tend to agree—; Neutral—; Tend to disagree—;
    Disagree—

    If this were to come about, do you feel that for American education it would be:

    Advantageous—; Tend to be advantageous—; Neutral—;
    Tend to be disadvantageous—; Disadvantageous—

5. The impact of Head Start and other programs for the disadvantaged

will provide such opportunities that this group will be able to take their rightful place in the educational stream by the time of their college years.

Agree___; Tend to agree___; Neutral___; Tend to disagree___; Disagree___

6. During the decade ahead we will have available innumerable methods for judging the qualities of college environments and the personal styles of applicants; this should markedly increase the effectiveness of the admissions process.

Agree___; Tend to agree___; Neutral___; Tend to disagree___; Disagree___

If this were to come about, do you feel that for American education it would be:

Advantageous___; Tend to be advantageous___; Neutral___; Tend to be disadvantageous___; Disadvantageous___

Part II. The following eight questions are drawn from a study on the applicants to 43 colleges, the names of which are listed below. (Where choices of answers are not given, write in your best estimate.)

1. How many applications did the average candidate to these colleges file to this group of 43? _____

2. What percentage of these candidates filed more than three applications to these colleges? _____

3. What is the relationship between the selectivity of a college to which an applicant applies and the number of applications he makes?
   Selectivity has little relationship to number of applications filed _____
   If selectivity is high, the number of applications is large _____
   If selectivity is low, the number of applications is large _____

4. Public school candidates make more _____ fewer _____ applications than private school candidates.

5. Those candidates with high scores make more _____ fewer _____ applications than those with low scores.

6. What percentage of candidates receive three or more admissions tickets? _____

164

7. How much more important for admissions is it to have a 700+ score than a 500-600 SAT-V score?

    Increases the odds 5 times _____

    Increases the odds 3 times _____

    Increases the odds 2 times _____

    Increases the odds negligibly _____

8. How much more important for admissions is it to have attended private school than public school?

    Three times as important _____

    Twice as important _____

    Is of no advantage _____

    Is a handicap _____

Alfred	Carleton	Grinnell	Princeton	Tufts
Amherst	Chicago	Hamilton	Reed	Union
Antioch	Clarkson	Harvard	R.P.I. (N.Y.)	U. of Cal.
Bates	Colby	Haverford	Rice	(Berkeley)
Bowdoin	Colgate	Lafayette	Rochester	U. of Penn.
Brown	Columbia	Lehigh	Stanford	Wesleyan
Bucknell	Cornell	M.I.T.	Swarthmore	Williams
Cal. Tech.	Dartmouth	Oberlin	Syracuse	Yale
Carnegie	Duke	Pomona	Trinity (Conn.)	

A Look from the Twenty-first Century

George H. Hanford

In the early stages of my research for this assignment, when I was going through some of the old dead files in the subbasement of the College Board's office building in New York, I happened upon a misplaced folder, marked in ink with a quavering hand, "Undelivered Speeches— 1987." Believing that we in the twenty-first century could profit from the wisdom of the twentieth, I opened the folder. It contained a single, handwritten manuscript headed "Reminiscences of a College Board Employee: 1967–1987," with an explanatory subtitle that read "Remarks prepared for delivery by Testy Ceeb, Curator of Records, on the occasion of his retirement from the College Entrance Examination Board, June 23, 1987." Without even stopping to sign the folder out, I clutched these hallowed, yellowed pages from the past to my breast and beat a hasty retreat to the privacy of my own office. There, behind locked doors, the past came alive as I turned the pages of that long-forgotten manuscript. And as the past came alive, my research effort ceased, for where else could one find a more accurate record of what happened in the years after 1967 than that prepared, in his own hand, by the Board's own Curator of Records.

And so what readers will be seeing is not an original work of mine, but another's words from the distant past, not in the old English of that bygone era but in the modern idiom as translated and transcribed from the original manuscript by the DO-RE-DOUBLE-TRANS *at* ETS—*that is, by the Document Reader, Translator, and Transcribing Machine at the Electronic Transformation Senter (sic) at Vassarhaven.*

A lot has happened to the College Board since I joined the staff some 20 years ago—since that first colloquium I attended; and Hanford's crystal ball was then, as my memory is now, certainly pretty clouded. And yet, with the IRIS—that's the Information Retrieval Electronic Synthesizer—on the fritz at the moment, my notes and memory of that occasion are the only benchmarks I have for assessing progress.

As I think back over the multitude of documents and the myriad of tapes that have come across my desk and my scanner—against the backdrop of that "Happening at Interlochen" some 20 years ago—it would seem to me that all admissions problems can be classified as one of three types: transient tribulations, everlasting verities, or timeless tensions. As my parting shot, I'd like to talk with you today about a modicum of each.

First of all, let me remind you of some of the transient tribulations that beset the admissions community a generation ago—some of the temporary problems that, while they loomed large on the admissions scene in 1967, have long since disappeared. For instance, there was great concern over the variety of transcript and other paper forms used in the admissions process. In retrospect, what a ridiculous matter to have spent so much time on, when today we don't shuffle papers at all! We just let the school, college, and College Board computers communicate with each other about candidates.

Or that whole mishmash of problems involving admissions-officer contacts with students and counselors—having to do with interviews, on campus and off; campus tours and school visits; catalogs and view books; college days and nights; days in the air and nights on the road. If only the rugged heroes and hardy heroines of that era had been able to glimpse the future and see how students today can visit colleges by television without leaving school. How an admissions officer can tape his spiel once a year and have it available to groups of students across the land at the push of a button. How student and counselor and admissions officer can sit at the visu-phone, each in his own natural habitat, and preserve that close intimate relationship among themselves that everybody thought 20 years ago the electronic age was going to destroy.

Or what about the meeting fever that everyone complained about in those days—the excessive number of profession-related gatherings that admissions directors, and everybody else, had annually to attend from coast to coast. Again, the electronic age has come to our rescue. We can sit peacefully in the office and watch the meetings on television or go down to the local communications center and participate in the proceedings over the two-way, closed circuit channels, as so many of you are doing in this 1987 reincarnation of Interlochen.

Of one tribulation that is thankfully at last proving to be transient I would not treat as lightly. Even though we have not yet completely won the war on poverty, we have in the past 20 years come a long way in learning how to eliminate its deadening effects on the educational achievements and aspirations of youngsters affected by low socioeconomic status and cultural deprivation. But this is a matter to which I will return later.

But enough of these problems of a bygone era. In retrospect, except for the last, all were but interesting annoyances in a primitive period of college admissions. They were not at all significant for the long-range perception of the process of access to higher education, for what we call today accommodation to postsecondary opportunity.

Then there are the everlasting verities of college admissions, the insoluble problems of the profession. My first three examples are taken pretty much from the world of the College Board itself.

Verity the first: Whether the College Board should test English composition by asking students to compose English will never be satisfactorily decided. The outward manifestations will change, but not the fundamental issue. Twenty years ago the alternatives were to write with a pencil in a blue book or stroke between two lines on an answer sheet. Today, they are a light pencil or a button on a machine console. In the Interlochen era, the reliability of the readers was in question; today, it is the reliability of the instructions given to different document scanners that grade what the light pencils write.

Verity the second: Students and their counselors will always complain about score changes between exposures on College Board tests. In 1967, people questioned the difficulty level of two versions of the Scholastic Aptitude Test, usually, the comparability between the March and December administrations of a given year. Today, they question the wiring of the two consoles at which a student punches his buttons.

Verity the third: College Board test dates will always be unsatisfactory to somebody. A generation ago, the burning issue was whether the then proposed November date would interfere with interscholastic football games. Today, Johnny's problem is that the testing consoles are all scheduled during the school days for the next month and he can get access to one only on the night of the dramatic club performance.

Verity the fourth: Coaches and athletic directors, like influential alumni and public officials, will always be thorns in the admissions office side. Despite that classic foundation study made in the early 1970s on athletic recruiting and influence wielding—the one formally called "The Evil Use of Cleats and Shoehorns in College Admissions"—and despite other similar abortive efforts, I think you would all agree that there hasn't been an iota of progress in the last 20 years. And anybody who thinks that things are going to change in the next 20 is, in my opinion, nuts!

Well, these are but four of the everlasting verities. I'm sure that you can think of more: like the fact that there will be eternal controversy over computation of rank in class, despite the international effort in this regard that accompanied the introduction of the world-wide, language-

168

free SAT in the early 1980s; or that the constant ebb and flow of curricular change and the tides of subject matter reform will ever be; or that the debate over the question of whether a school should be asked to recommend a student to a college will never end. But these are matters about which little can be done. They are eternal truths *with* which admissions officers of every generation must live to learn and learn to live and yet *about* which they must never expect to be able to do anything of lasting significance.

As you can see, I have assigned the transient tribulations and everlasting verities of college admissions to the realm of relative insignificance as far as the 20 years from 1967 to 1987 have been concerned. Not that they could actually have been ignored; they were too real for that. It's just that the responses of the admissions community to what I call the timeless tensions were what really characterized those two decades.

In the presence of this knowledgeable audience, I shall not even attempt to interpret where we stand along the continuums that connect the pairs of polar positions between which most of the timeless tensions stretch, for your own individual judgments would be as valid as mine. And anyway this celebration of my retirement is an occasion for some nostalgic reminiscences about past events, not for a critical evaluation of current status.

In the abstract, I find that most of my timeless tensions can be comprehended between two all-encompassing polar positions that I would mundanely call centralization and decentralization. Certainly, the major topic of debate in education over the last 20 years has been how much more federal control should follow ever-increasing federal aid to education—a debate that can be comprehended between the centralized pole of federal control and the decentralized pole of local control of education. I do not need to remind this audience of recent developments in this regard, of their effects on the process of accommodation to postsecondary education, and of the role of the College Board in attempting to preserve the process as a prerogative of the educational enterprise and in trying to keep it from becoming a function of the governmental establishment.

But as benchmarks for your own evaluation of progress since 1967, let me remind you of two of Hanford's general predictions: First, that, as universal secondary education followed on the heels of universal primary education and as universal postsecondary is following universal secondary education, so may we expect that the next stage will be universal opportunity for graduate study—and that the stage after that will be universal adult education.

There follows in the manuscript an unfinished parenthetical comment that the curator at first felt compelled to try to compose and then, apparently on second thought, decided to cross out. As best I can make it out, he had thought of saying: "As I approach my golden years and the afterlife, I wonder why Hanford stopped there. Why not continuing education for the senior citizen and universal opportunity for"—and here is where he seems to have run into trouble—"universal opportunity for eternal education . . . No, that's religion. Universal preparation for the afterlife . . . No, that's the prerogative of Purgatory. Education not a panacea . . . need faith . . ."

The curator didn't even bother to close the parentheses, but from the perspective of the twenty-first century, it is interesting to observe how, in his halting, intuitive way, he foresaw the world-wide religious revival that ushered in this century. He realized that education and faith can together do a better job of saving mankind than either one alone, just as I suppose he realized that the school record and test scores could together do a better job of predicting college grades than either one alone.

The unstruck text continues with the curator's report of Hanford's second general prediction.

Second, that primary education will remain essentially under truly local control; that secondary education will more and more be regionally governed; that state master plans will determine the course of undergraduate education; that national purpose will be served and national human resources preserved by what may not be called, but by what will in effect be, a national master plan for graduate and professional education—but that continuing, adult education will remain a matter of individual right to partake voluntarily at secondary, undergraduate, or graduate levels.

How right he was about the tensions that were created. There was the temptation on the one hand to turn all the problems of accommodation to postsecondary opportunity over to public authority and to leave to regional secondary boards and state higher education authorities the task of creating their own conjunctions. On the other hand was the challenge to the admissions community to keep the responsibility and its attendant frustrations unto itself, the challenge of maintaining a national mobility for students entering college—their right to go down

170

state or across a continent—when, of course, more and more of them were beginning higher education down the street or across town.

More specifically, Hanford, you will recall, spent the late 1960s bleating about cooperative admissions ventures. His theory was that interinstitutional cooperation in any form, however meager, was better than the rugged individualism that colleges then practiced in the admissions process, better than their excessive application of the right to institutional autonomy in the practice of college entrance procedures. I've often wondered if Hanford were surprised at the accommodation that has been made between the timeless tensions of common or centrally polarized procedures and diverse or decentralized ones in accommodating students to postsecondary opportunity.

There follows at this point a quotation within a quotation attributed, in the single footnote the curator made in his entire manuscript, to some character who seems to have been named Ibid. Because of an inability to determine the approximate date of composition, it has been impossible to give the proper translating instructions to the DO-RE-DOUBLE-TRANS, *and so I present the quote to you in its original form.*

"And it came to pass that there lived in those days a major prophet named David of Cambridge, called the Ries-man, a sociologist by profession. David spake of many things and among them of the snake-like academic procession—from its Ivy League front to its open door end.

"And to David there was a minor disciple named Ibid, the pseudo-psalmist, who sang of the progress of the procession through the stages of admissions.

'Early on a warm body, a full pocketbook,
    and the right credentials would get you there.
But then the numbers began to grow
    and how good your credentials came to bear.

'Later on how bright was not enough.
You had to be made of other stuff.
First, to reside somewhere afar,
And then be well-rounded in the extracurricular.

'But then the well-rounded lad
    because his radius was small
    began to look dull after all.

'So attention turned in filling the void

171

To the concept known as the oblate spheroid.
To the lad, mostly well-round still, but wait,
Who possessed as well some special skill or trait
Like his way with math, his speed of foot,
His eye for music or the basketball hoop,
—The rocket he made not just for fun
—Or the pile he'll raise for the alumni fund
... the nation of his kin
... or the color of his skin.' "

There is at this point a marginal note—along the edge of the manuscript. "Definition of well-rounded by Radcliffe Heermance, director of admissions at Princeton in the 1930s and 1940s: The quintessence of 'well-roundedness' is the billiard ball. It takes on a high polish and is easily pushed around."

In speaking thus of the admissions procession, our pseudopsalmist was, I believe, trying to say two things: first that *in* his time, there were colleges whose interest ran the gamut from the warm body to the oblate spheroid; but, second and more important, that *over* time, the values of colleges are bound to change in response to the timeless tensions among societal demands, institutional aspirations, faculty interests, and student needs. And as college values change, their admissions policies change with them in some implicit, undefined way. I remember Hanford, for instance, making the point that his alma mater first wanted bright students in order to be a strong educational institution, then sought a nationally representative student body to reassert its national role, but then worried about getting too intellectual to be a vigorous leader, and discovered that leadership does not always come in well-rounded packages. These are partial descriptions of its goals and values that Harvard would probably not happily have accepted; but Harvard perceives itself as a leader and, in its admissions policy, appears to have reflected its perception of the changing needs of its leadership role as far as students are concerned.

At Interlochen 20 years ago, Hanford suggested that the process of describing institutions was not only primitive by future standards, but even more primitive than the then-existing means of describing individuals. You may recall further that he predicted that the then-current student call for relevance in education would have the ultimate effect of forcing higher institutions to reevaluate their goals and values. They would have to translate those goals and values into meaningful descrip-

172

tions, into profiles that students could interpret and understand. I'll not presume to evaluate the validity of Hanford's prediction for you, but I can't refrain from a few examples:

In the 1950s, there was a societal interest in the egghead that affected college aspirations. In the early 1960s, in response to the civil rights movement, there was a major recruiting effort for able Negroes. In the late 1960s, there was the student call for relevance, which prompted *some* colleges to seek docile, convergent thinkers and *others* to seek the potential troublemakers. In the 1970s, there was the faculty call for putting teaching back in the classroom, and the admissions search for heterogeneity.

Or, from more recent experience, let me remind you of what's happened to the concept of a community college. Twenty years ago, in 1967, a community college was almost by definition an open-door, two-year institution offering terminal, technical, and transfer programs. As a result of the movement in the early 1980s to put the "community" back in community colleges, these institutions were, by and large, forced to a choice between remaining two-year in character and preparatory in function—preparing the younger age groups for work, or adult life, or an upper-division program—and becoming centers for continuing education for all the community. You'll have to admit that the admissions policies and procedures of these two types of institutions are today quite different.

In my 20 years with the College Board, I think I have seen some hopeful signs of progress toward the enunciation of the differing goals and values of higher education and their translation into reasonable admissions policies and practices.

I can perhaps best summarize what I am trying to say by talking for a moment about the question of whether the admissions community has played a vigorous or forceful enough role in that translation. Has the admissions officer had a say in the determination as well as the translation, or has he just listened?

The manuscript breaks off suddenly at this point, as if somehow our curator–emeritus could not bring himself to the point of evaluation and summary he had promised. But there is a hint of what he might have said in two typewritten pages attached to the manuscript, pages that, after carbon analysis, would appear to date from 1967 itself and are probably Xerox excerpts from Hanford's paper at that Interlochen colloquium.

173

The first page contains what I would call a mid-twentieth-century parable, appropriately titled Appendix A.

And it came to pass that the admissions director went up out of the vineyards and into the house of the president, went up out of the land of athletic directors, alumni sons, and state legislators, out of the fields of recruitment and selection. Yea, up he went, out of the morass of folders and statistics and the darkness of ghosts and late bloomers, up he went into the presence of the president.

When he had come and the president had seen the gloom that was upon this man whom he had hired, he said, "Come with me to the Ivory Tower of my abode and see the brightness of the future." And they went together into the elevator and ascended into the uppermost reaches of the Tower. There the president faced the admissions director toward the future and cried, "Behold!" And the admissions director replied, "But, Sire, I see naught but the railing which is at my hand."

Whereupon the president said, "Take off your glasses of day-to-day decisions and put on the spectacles of Thresher and Foresight." And he did and was amazed. And he asked his leader, "What means all this that I see around me?" And the president answered him saying, "Behind you lies the past. Before you, the future."

And the admissions director spread wide his arms and exclaimed, "But the future has so many roads leading off into it, from my left hand to my right."

And the president replied, "The pathway of the future is in your hands and mine. But it cannot be foretold from the present. It will be determined only by the direction you and I choose to walk tomorrow."

Here endeth the parable of Appendix A.

The second typewritten page also appears to have been a Xerox copy of a page from Hanford's 1967 Interlochen paper. From its nature, I would assume it to be the last page. Before reading it to you, however, I would note that for some strange reason it starts in parabolic language, shifts gradually to an idiom not uncommon in our present day, and ends with words spoken at a 1957 College Board colloquium.

As I compose these words, my days of acting draweth to a close. [*Here he would seem to be making reference not to his most meager dramatic talents, but to the fact of his being acting president of the College Board while President Richard Pearson was on leave.*] My days of acting, like unto the contents of this paper, draw thankfully to a close. Would that I could in fact have foretold the future as the colloquium

174

planning committee had envisaged and that I could have responded clearly to their query, "What do you see ahead in college admissions policies and problems?"

Like the admissions officer of Appendix A, I see many pathways to the future. Some are but aimless side roads into the realm of transient tribulations; others, but winding lanes leading into the land of everlasting verities. But I can see important pathways, too, stretching out from my right hand to my left. These are pathways of opportunity for institutional decisions about purposes and values *only in support of which* can college admissions policies and practices in the final analysis effectively be determined.

Because I believe that its diversity is one of the great strengths of the American educational enterprise, I hope that the pathways chosen will be many and that they will be chosen with Thresher and Foresight, with true regard both for the general public interest and for individual institutional purpose. As for the admissions community within that total enterprise, I hope I can see time and effort devoted not to exploration of the side roads and winding lanes but to direct and active participation in the translation of the values of our society into meaningful definitions of the varied purposes of higher education. For, in words spoken by Edward K. Graham at a colloquium at Arden House in 1957, "How a college or university goes about selecting a student body is directly or indirectly a reflection of all the purposes which the college or university serves, the values which it regards as most important, and in no uncertain sense, is the real measure of the genius or spirit of the place."[1]

---

1. *Planning College Policy for the Critical Decade Ahead.* New York: College Entrance Examination Board, 1958, p. 71.